HAWAIIAN ORDEAL

UKRAINIAN
CONTRACT
WORKERS

1897 - 1910

*Michael
Ewanchuk*

Michael Ewanchuk 1908—

Hawaiian Ordeal: Ukrainian Contract Workers 1897-1910
1. Literary - Artistic
2. Ukraine - Hawaii - Manchuria
3. Canada - United States
4. Sugar Cane Plantation Contract Workers
5. Immigration - settlements

ISBNO-9690768-6-x (hard cover)
ISBNO-9690768-7-8 (limp cover)

Michael Ewanchuk, Publisher, Winnipeg, Manitoba

Printed by Derksen Printers, Steinbach, Manitoba

To the Descendants Of Ukrainian
Immigrants in North America

ACKNOWLEDGMENTS

To all those who during the research period and the writing of *Hawaiian Ordeal* have so willingly provided assistance, information and guidance, I wish to express my sincere thanks.

My special thanks go to the Interlake and Gimli Ukrainian Historical Society, Tony Kuz, president; W.P. Solypa, Peter Onysko, Rev. John A. Melnyk and the late Mr. Peter Humeniuk, members of the executive, who encouraged me to write this book.

For the information originally provided by my late brother, John of Chicago, I wish to express my appreciation.

I am grateful to the archivists of the National Archives, Washington, D.C., and the State Archives of Hawaii, Honolulu; to the librarians of the Library of Congress, the University of Hawaii, Honolulu; the Public Library of Hilo, Hi.; the Public Library at Lahaina, Maui; and to the kind lady of the Hawaii State Archives, whose name unfortunately got misplaced, who directed us to the descendants of the contract workers on the Big Island. I am also grateful to Mr. Michael Lizak and Mrs. Helen Richardson of Mountain View, and the Verbiske family of Volcano, P.O., Hi for sharing information and documents; Mr. Andrew Sorokowski of San Francisco, The Yakimishyn family, Mr. Frank A. Dubenski of Winnipeg, my good friend, Isidore Goresky of Edmonton for helping me establish contact with people and providing data.

For the assistance in the preparation of maps, I wish to express my sincere appreciation to the Geography Department, University of Winnipeg and to Prof. John C. Lehr.

And finally, I am deeply indebted to the Taras Shevchenko Foundation in Winnipeg for the financial assistance, else the author would have had to bear the total cost of publishing the *Hawaiian Ordeal: Ukrainian Contract Workers 1897-1910.*

TABLE OF CONTENTS

FOREWORD

In his new book, *Hawaiian Ordeal*, Michael Ewanchuk takes us back to the last decade of the 19th century when the Ukrainians on their way to "America" signed contracts of indenture to work on sugar cane plantations in Hawaii. Their experiences in the "Paradise Isles of the Pacific" were, however, far from happy: they were maltreated and exploited. Yet after the first group of 1897 arrived, the agents managed to induce more to come, and later they were joined by a much larger group of displaced farmers from the Ukrainian steppes who were sent to Manchuria. In Hawaii

both groups wree forced by Hackfeld (head of a sugar conglomerate) and other planters to work under "near-slave" conditions.

In his Hawaiian "saga" the author gives due space to the other contract workers, the Chinese, the Poles, the Japanese, the Russians and the Portugese and also to the brave Norwegians who also experienced intolerable conditions of work and treatment. To show the difficulties the people had to endure, Mr. Ewanchuk provides some details about travel around Cape Horn, South America, in a German sailboat with a captain very much of Captain Bligh's ilk. The study is based not only on extensive research in the archives and libraries, but also on two visits to the Islands and interviews with the descendants of the first group of contract workers of 1897-1900, who still live in Hawaii. His study is an excellent historical research which is buttressed with documents, maps, quotations, and translations from reliable sources.

Mr. Ewanchuk, a descendant of Ukrainian pioneers, Wasyl and Paraskiva Ewanchuk, of the Gimli area fully understands and appreciates the problems of pioneer life. He understands why the Ukrainians who went to Hawaii would eventually give up their homesteads in the Olaa Rain Forest Reserve to go to Canada to acquire homesteads in the parkland areas of Western Canada, or to find new life in the industrial areas of United States once they were released from the state of servitude and inhumane treatment when their contracts were abrogated.

The author was born and received his elementary and high school education in Gimli, Manitoba and his Grade XII in the United College while in residence at the P. Mohyla Institute. He attended the Detroit Institute of Technology and the Detroit City College (Now Wayne University). This he was able to do while working nights at the Ford plant. On returning to Winnipeg, he became a teacher, school principal and a school inspector. He has a good knowledge of Ukrainian language - but, claims a "reading

vii

knowledge" only of other languages - consequently he is able to appraise and translate documents he needs for his work.

He received his B.A., B.Ed., and M.Ed., degrees from the University of Manitoba, and the Canadian College of Teachers recognized his work with a Fellowship, F.C.C.T. In 1977 the University of Winnipeg granted him an honorary degree of Doctor of Laws.

The late, Dr. V.J. Kaye, archivist and Ukrainian historian rated Dr. Ewanchuk's work as essayist and researcher as being of high quality; and in appraising his progress observed:

> His dedication to work in the field of education brought him well earned recognition. In 1958-59 the Manitoba Inspectors' Association elected him president. In 1960 he was elected president of the Alumni Association of the University of Manitoba; in 1968 he became Dominion president of the Canadian Association of School Superintendents and Inspectors.

The Ukrainian Canadian Committee in commemorating 90 years of Ukrainian settlement in Canada awarded him a special certificate of recognition.

The author of *Hawaiian Ordeal*, an erstwhile factory worker, school teacher, R.C.A.F. Flight Lieutenant, and School Inspector has in a short time since his retirement from "active duties" written and published four outstanding books about Ukrainian settlements in Western Canada. *Hawaiian Ordeal* adds a new dimension to his work and is a signficant contribution to Canadian writing. As an experienced statistician, he has limited the scope of his research concentrating on the Ukrainian laborers and the Islands of Hawaii. The Hawaiians have a new addition to their history and the descendants of Ukrainian settlers in the New World and the readers at large have a fine opportunity to read about the venturesome people who in time of distress were fortunate to be able to depend on their clergy in the New World, and in particular on the journalist-clergyman, Iwan Ardan, editor of "Svoboda", to be able to cast-off their shackles of indenture.

Mr. Tony Kuz,
Department of Geography,
University of Winnipeg,
May 1, 1986.

PREFACE

It was the distinguished Ukrainian journalist, the late Luke Myshuha, who in the thirties got the writer interested in the plight of the Ukrainian contract workers - who for years toiled on the Hawaiian plantations under near-slave conditions and wanted me to investigate their experiences by travelling from Detroit, Michigan to Hawaii to prepare a report on their life there and also that of Dr. N. K. Russel, the first Ukrainian to arrive in Hawaii in 1892, and who was eventually elected to the Hawaiian senate. He was of the opinion that a report on the life of contract workers in the "Paradise of the Pacific" would be a fitting contribution to the first issue of the "Ukrainian Weekly" he was planning to publish in the English language.

Through the years the writer tried to collect only material that was available, but it was not until 1975 that it was possible to carry out the research in the State Archives in Honolulu and the Bishop Museum. However, the disappointing thing was the relative materials in print or any artifacts in the Museum that would record the coming and the life of the people from Ukraine in Hawaii were hard to find or were non-existent.

After extensive correspondence, however, and a trip to the National Archives in Washington and the Library of Congress, it was possible to find pertinent materials, more so, about the group that came to Hawaii from Manchuria; and their object in coming appeared the same as those who came from Western Ukraine: to gain wider freedom and to locate on land.

In 1985 the researcher decided to make another trip to Hawaii, this time to trace the descendants of the original groups of 1897-1899 and the groups that started to come from their settlements in Asia from around Harbin, in 1909. With the assistance of the librarians in the Hilo Library and the people in the State Archives in Honolulu, it was possible to find several descendants in the Hilo area at Mountain View.

* * * * *

After evaluating the available material about the Ukrainians in Hawaii, and analyzing the conditions of work of the contract workers in the Islands, the writer has put the information into a book. The *Hawaiian Ordeal: Ukrainian Contract Workers, 1897-1910* is, therefore, the result of an 11-year study about the brave Ukrainians, and other Europeans who, like the Chinese, Japanese, Portuguese and other contract workers before them, suffered untold miseries on the Hawaiian sugar cane plantations from the planters and their cow-whip-wielding-sadistic lunas.

M.E.

Winnipeg, Manitoba
May 1, 1986

INTRODUCTION

It staggers one's imagination to learn that in 1897 peasants from Central Europe would dare to leave their native land — a country rich in natural resources and very favorable Continental climate — and travel across the oceans to seek land, freedom and employment in the distant Pacific Islands of Hawaii. The emigration of Ukrainian people from Western Ukraine to Hawaii is a fascinating study and has a romantic touch to it; more so since this migration entailed a four-month voyage by sailboat around the Horn. And the voyage around the Horn was in those days dreaded even by the more seasoned sailors. Yet these pilgrims seemed to be impelled by the opportunities promised them to be able to establish a better future for themselves and their children.

This study becomes more interesting and widens one's historical perspective when one learns that there was another wave of Ukrainians who even before 1897 left in a different direction and eventually reached Hawaii. These were the peasants from Greater Ukraine — from the lands around Poltava, Kiev and Odessa who were virtually forced out of their paternal homes by the Russians to make room for settlers from Germany and for the German entrepreneurs. Some of these crossed the bleak stretches of Siberia to reach the Far East; others sailed by way of the Black Sea, the Red Sea and the Indian Ocean to reach the Yellow Sea and Mukden and then turned inland establishing settlements at Harbin and along the Amur river, but mainly in the Ussuri river basin. These settlements along with those of other people from Russia were to form a bulwark against the northern expansion of the Chinese. And eventually these Ukrainians went to Hawaii to work on sugar cane plantations and each group in turn passed through the primitive experience of the "Hawaiian Ordeal" in the land of the former dynasty of King Kamehameha. Little did the people know that in signing contracts in Bremerhaven or in Harbin in Manchuria, that they endentured themselves to the sugar magnates of Hawaii, and virtually became their slaves for a period of three or five years, as the case may have been. They not only placed themselves in bondage, but also their children. But they were not alone; there were Oriental, Filippino, Portugese and other contract laborers who experienced the same difficulties on arrival in the Islands; for in bondage people of all creeds and "races" become equal.

True the Ukrainians from Manchuria arrived in Hawaii some 12 years later than those from Western Ukraine who sailed around the Horn, but they arrived in greater numbers. Though they experienced the same ordeal, they adopted a different mode of attack to extricate themselves from the new state of peonage in Hawaii — peonage akin to that their Cossack forebearers suffered under the Romanovs; and the burden of our story is to show how these exiles from Ukraine bore their yoke in Hawaii.

Through the years the sugar industry developed and the entrepreneurs of Europe prospered in the distant Islands by exploiting the land of the native Hawaiians and the labor of the contract workers they imported into the Islands. This exploitation and abuse of contract workers appear to exist even today, but in the different islands. The International Labour Office* in recent years has brought to light the exploitation of the Haitian contract laborers by some sugar cane plantation owners in the Dominican Republic.

To assure a full complement of labor in the sugar cane fields, Haitians entering the Dominican Republic clandestinely are rounded up by military personnel and transported to work on the plantations under threat of deportation.

We learn further that these workers "often put in 15-hour days, under broiling sun with only water and sugar cane to sustain them while they work." Workers are paid on the basis of tonnage of cane they cut, but this tonnage is greatly reduced as the cane is left to dry, and since it is also weighed when the workers are not present, there is evidence that "cheating takes place." In addition to these excesses, the contract workers have to buy their supplies and food in the stores on the plantations where high prices are charged. In their living compound the International Labor Office reports, there is no running water or electricity and the sanitary conditions are deplorable. The laborers are also forebidden to leave the plantations.

Therefore, it appears, that these laborers are unable to have any savings after a stretch of a six-month heavy work ordeal; consequently, when one expects that through the years action has been taken to ameliorate working conditions and improve wages for the laborers on the sugar plantations, they remain unchanged.

In this study we shall use the case of Ukrainian contract workers in Hawaii to discuss in more detail the horrible experiences of the laborers in the "Paradise Islands".

---

* Vol. 19, No. 4, October 1983.

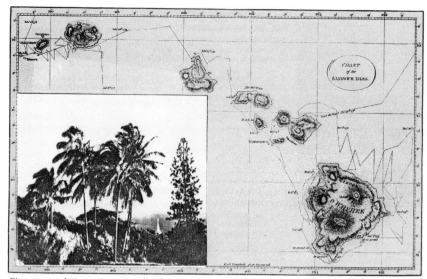

First map of Hawaii, originally drawn by Captain William Bligh, reproduced in 1784.

(Lahaina Printsellers)

List of Maps

Other books by Michael Ewanchuk

A History of the Ukrainian Settlements in the Gimli Area (in Ukrainian), 1975.

Vita: A Ukrainian Community (a set of three books), 1977.

Spruce, Swamp and Stone: A History of the Pioneer Ukrainian Settlements in the Gimli Area, 1977.

Pioneer Profiles: Ukrainian Settlers in Manitoba, 1981.

PART I

From Bremerhaven to Honolulu

KAUAI

Lihue

OAHU
Honolulo

MOLOKAI

Lahina

MAUI

HAWAII
(Big Island)

Hilo

Kona

Mt. View

Kau

Hawaiian Islands.

Rev. Iwan Wolonsky Professor Joseph Oleskow (PAC)
(Jubilee Book, U.N.A 1936)

teacher by training, was chosen to accompany the first organized group to preclude any attempt by agents to bilk them of their resources or to dissuade them from going to Canada.

Rev. Iwan Wolansky and Prof. Joseph Oleskow, therefore, must be given full credit as both influenced the course of Ukrainian emigration and influenced the settlement of the Canadian West.

Port Agents

The actions taken by Prof. Oleskow did much to inform the people emigrating to the New World and they began to be wary of the machinations of the port agents. However, there were many who were less informed about the activities of the various extortionists in the German ports and they fell for the deceptions expounded. The German port agents notably Missler and Morowitz, not only collected a bonus[1] of $5.00 for each Ukrainian, or other European settler travelling to Canada, but they and their sub-agents also resorted to various forms of extortion. Leopold Carlo reports:

> He (the agent) also used the alarm clock to ask the "American Emperor" whether he would permit the particular emigrant to enter. For this assurance, an extra fee was charged. When a swindler, dressed as a doctor, refused to qualify a perspective emigrant, the emigrant was advised to bribe the fake medical examiner. Even peasant dress received special attention; the emigrants were in-

---

[1] John. C. Lehr, "The Process and Pattern of Ukrainian Rural Settlement in Western Canada, 1891-1914," unpublished doctoral thesis, University of Manitoba, Winnipeg, 1978., p. 50.

formed that those in peasant clothing would not be admitted to America. Lowenberg, one of this syndicate, had a store full of clothing for this purpose.[2]

Consequently, immigrants outfitted in the Lowenberg establishment, often arrived in the New Land looking like scarecrows wearing clothing of Bavarian peasants or Tyrolean highlanders and were ridiculed and criticized.

By the spring of 1897, large groups of settlers from various Ukrainian villages were leaving for Canada where they were to become known as Sifton's settlers. They were travelling unsponsored paying their own travel expenses and thus were free to select land in any area of Western Canada open for homesteading and become independent farmers. The steamship companies were alert to the business significance of the immigrant travel and anxious to provide the required transportation across the Ocean for the new settlers. The agents, however, monitored the movement of the groups from the time they began to leave their Ukrainian villages, then met them as they arrived in the port cities and tried to influence them where to go.

During the winter of 1897, one group of 34 families from the district of Borschiw in Western Ukraine left for Canada. This group reached Bremen without any difficulties; and in Bremen they were met by one F. Missler, an agent for the North-German Steamship Company Line.[3]

"New Jerusalem" Instead of Canada

In Bremen, Missler suggested to the prospective Canadian settlers that they go to another country, which in comparison to Canada was a "New Jerusalem". This "New Jerusalem" was a country unknown to them. It was Hawaii.

Missler started to dissuade them from going to Canada, but instead urged them to go to the Hawaiian Islands; telling them that their work was less onerous, the wages were much better and the climate mild and less subject to extremes. And the immigrants believed him and signed the contracts presented to them, not realizing that by doing so they were indenturing themselves to work in the Hawaiian sugar plantations for a period of three years and thus placing themselves totally under the control of the sugar cane planters.[4]

As an agent Missler became known for his unscrupulous approaches in order to fill his quotas of workers and settlers for the steamship companies and countries utilizing his services.

The Ukrainian paper "Svoboda"[5] in reporting about the Ukrainian laborers going to Hawaii decried the fact fearing that they may be deluded like the

---

[2] Henry T.K. Dutkiewicz, "Some aspects of Polish Peasant Immigration to North America from Austrian Poland between the years 1863 and 1910", unpublished masters thesis, University of Ottawa, 1958. (Microfilm).

[3] Yar Chyz, "Narodna Vola Almanac", Scranton, Pa. 1926. (The Jar Chyz essay is based on a "Svoboda" article of 1897).

[4] Ibid. p. 83.

[5] Svoboda, M. Carmel, Pa. 1897.

settlers whom Missler persuaded earlier to go to Argentine.

In dissuading the settlers from going to Canada, Missler had written letters to the peasants in the Ukraine who sought information about emigration to the "New World". J.C. Lehr in his doctoral thesis quotes a section from one of those letters.

> It is true that in Canada one may get free land, but this is of no value; being located in cold regions where heavy frosts prevail for seven months a year, where is also a lack of roads and people are isolated from one another.[6]

At the time of writing Missler was getting, no doubt, a much higher per capita commission for the settlers he recruited for Argentine than he could get if they emigrated to Canada; besides, he faced very strong competition from another agent of like ilk, Morowitz, who seemed to have closer working arrangements with steamship companies who were transporting settlers that were going to Canada.

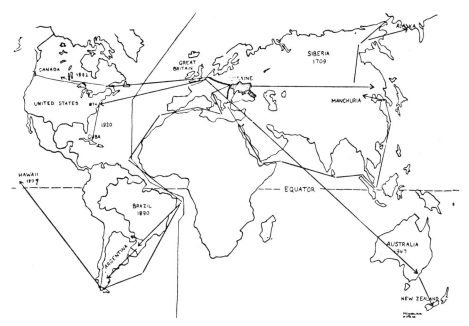

Map showing continents and countries to which Ukrainians immigrated.

---

[6] J.C. Lehr, op. cit., p. 113.

Chapter 2

First Group of Ukrainian Contract Workers
Travel to Hawaii

In 1897 a group of Ukrainian laborers who signed contracts in Bremen to work on sugar cane plantations in Hawaii, did not realize the complexity of their venture. At that time, though, people of Central Europe knew little about the New World across the Atlantic — about such areas as the United States, Brazil and Canada; they, however, knew next to nothing about Hawaii, whether the islands were called Sandwich Islands or Hawaii. Their concept about the distance they would have to travel was not at all clear. On leaving their native villages, and being Canada bound, they expected similar situations in Hawaii: an opportunity to settle on land, that is, to get a homestead and secure employment. However, they failed to realize, and appreciate the fact that they signed contracts of indenture, and were under obligation to serve in Hawaii a full term of three years. They failed to realize, also, that they were to serve their new employers, actually masters, and be subjected to the archaic laws of King Kamehameha; as in 1897 Hawaii was not as yet in union with the United States of America. In brief, they were horribly deceived by the agents who extolled the beauty of the islands and the wonderful climate. In this respect the recruiting agents did not exaggerate that, in fact, in going to Hawaii they were going to a "New Jerusalem" but that was all.

The Ukrainians induced to go to Hawaii were, no doubt, happy when they signed their contracts and were looking forward to life in the "Paradise Islands." It is necessary to acknowledge that they were brave people, prepared to cross oceans and travel more than half-way around the world to reach a country where they hoped they would be free, able to accept available employment, and eventually settle on land, as promised, in a country with very favorable climatic conditions. Yes, these settlers destined for Hawaii were brave, but at the same time they were greatly deluded and somewhat naive; they accepted the "allurements" of the agent who worked hand and glove with the German steamship company to supply the requisite quota of workers for the Hawaiian planters. Though they started to go to Canada after being informed by Prof. Oleskow about the free lands there, but at the same time they disregarded his warning: "Beware of Agents!" They failed to request Prof. Oleskow to provide them with a capable leader like Karl Genik.

In 1897 the emigrants embarking from Europe were most unfortunate if they had to make the voyage by Austrian or German ships; for as a rule, if they had to wait a few days or a week for the sailing date, they were lodged in inferior hotels, taverns or lodging houses, where they were often cheated. They had to pay the high price demanded for accommodation or their baggage was seized. Then they were most unfortunate if they took third class passage.

Third class was located at the bottom (hold) of the ship, where cabins were small — immigrants complained about the food — rotten herrings, uncleaned potatoes, rancid lard, smelly meat, dirty water and unwashed dishes and cutlery — the lack of respect on the part of the stewards.[1]

Those travelling to Canada or the U.S.A. seemed to receive a little better accommodation and treatment, but those who were booked for South America received horrible accommodation and inhuman treatment. As a rule the passage cost 180 marks, and half the amount for children under twelve years of age. The cost to New York or Canada was 189 marks.[2]

The emigrants of 1897 did not just fall by chance into the hands of the Bremen extortionists; it seems that their movements from the time they left their native villages were monitored by special agents of F. Missler and Company. In Bremen after having manoeuvered the emigrants into going to Hawaii, he made every effort to make the travel to the Pacific islands appear legal, and created the impression that he was taking all actions for their protection.

Once the contracts were signed, and having found accommodation for the emigrants, he and his sub-agents "guarded them against contacts" with his competitors. Then the documentation of the travellers was carefully checked; their birth certificates were examined, and they had to produce another document — a "certificate of good moral standing" either from the parish priest or from an official of the municipal unit, "gminna". Before the contract forms were processed and signed, each adult male had to produce a document of military training. Then each male contract worker was issued, gratis, a billfold from Missler with the imprint of his address on it. (Gift — part of his promotional scheme).

Missler also arranged for more additional free advertising; for before the "expedition" of laborers left, they were asked to write letters to their peo-

Gift Packet
—(Courtesy of Helen Richardson of Mountain View, Hawaii)

---

[1] Henry — T.K. Dutkiewicz, op.cit., p. 89 and passim.
[2] Ibid.

Andruch Werbicki's Certificate of Good Moral Character from Slobidka Dzhurynska, 28 March, 1897.
—(Courtesy of J. Verbiske (Werbicki), Volcano P.O. Hawaii).

Document showing military training of Petro Markiewicz of Kossow. Circa 1894.
—(Courtesy of Mrs. Helen Richardson).

ple at home informing them about the very favorable contracts they signed and they they were departing to a very fine country, a veritable Eden. Since some, like Panko Yakimishyn, had left their wives at home, they requested that Missler try to make arrangements to bring them to Hawaii, with the next expedition.

The Contract—"Kontrakt"[3]

On April 3, 1897 Andruch Werbicki signed a contract on behalf of himself and his family. Andruch Werbicki was either illiterate or could only write his name using the Ukrainian alphabet, and therefore, signed the contract with three x's. The document bore a "Hapalua", a Hawaiian duty stamp, to the value of $1.50 and was sealed with a stamp of the Consul of the Republic of Hawaii.

The contract shows that the laborer was destined to Onomea, just out of Hilo on the Big Island of Hawaii, and he and his family were provided with a free passage (steerage). Clause 1, also stipulated that food, lodging and medical care would be provided without charge to the place where he, Andruch Werbicki, would be employed as an agricultural laborer.

According to Clause 2, Andruch Werbicki agreed to accept such employment as assigned. Clause 3 stipulated that the wage was to be $18.00 per month for a 26 day month, but the laborer had to obey all lawful commands of the employer or his agents and overseers; work during the night and work on all days not recognized as holidays by Hawaiian Government. Therefore, Ukrainian laborers were not entitled to "Ukrainian" holidays — Christmas and Easter which they were used to celebrating according to the Julian calendar.

Unfurnished lodgings, fuel and water were to be provided on the plantations. Therefore, immediately on arrival the immigrant family had to acquire furnishings, a stove, and cooking utensils — all from the plantation stores, no doubt. All sections of the contract were made out in duplicate, and in three languages; English, German and Polish, except for the last section of the document, which was in English only - a language that Andruch Werbicki and others did not understand and this section was the most important; it established the relationship between Mr. Werbicki and the Onomea Sugar Co., placing him in the servant relationship to his Masters at Onomea, Hawaii.

It was a horrendous transaction which took advantage of Andruch Werbicki and others in a foreign country. They signed the "sworn" part of a covenent written in a language they did not understand (English) and without the advantages of legal counsel. In signing the contract, Andruch Werbicki committed not only himself to a state of bondage, but placed his whole family at a disadvantage in a strange country.

It is very doubtful whether the wife and children were present when Andruch Werbicki signed the contract on their behalf, and they they understood the contract. The representatives of the planters, therefore, perjured himself

---

[3] Courtesy of J. Verbiske (Werbicki), Volcano P.O., Hawaiian Island.

stipulations hereinafter contained to be kept and performed by the said laborer covenants and agrees as follows:

1. To furnish to the said laborer and his wife and 3 of his children, whose names and ages are noted at the bottom of this Agreement, free steerage passage, including proper food and medical attendance from **Bremerhaven** to **Honolulu** and also to produce proper lodgings for the said laborer and his family at **Honolulu**, proper transportation from Honolulu to the place where he is to be employed as an agricultural laborer.

2. On arrival at Honolulu the Employer agrees to provide employment for the said laborer as an agricultural laborer for the full period of three years, from the date such employment actually begins, and also proper employment for the wife and grown — up children of said laborer.

3. The employer guarantees to the said laborer wages at the rate of $ 18.— for each month of 26 days labor performed, and to his wife and grown — up children, if they desire to work, wages as follows:

To wives and daughters 20 years old for labor performed, wages at the rate of 40 cents pr. day

Daughters from 18 to 20 years	35	"	cents pr. day
" 16 " 18	30	"	
" 14 " 16	25	"	
Sons of 16 " 18	50	"	
" 14 " 16	40	"	
" 12 " 14	25	"	

and besides the wages the laborer is to have free of charge, for himself and family: unfurnished lodgings, also fuel and water for cooking, and medical attendance and medicine.

4. During the continuance of this contract the said laborer shall be free from all personal taxes, the Employer guarantees to him and his family

the full, equal, and perfect protection of the laws of the Hawaiian Islands, also free primary instructions in the Public Schools to his minor children.

The said laborer, in consideration of the stipulations hereinbefore mentioned, to be kept and performed by the employer, covenants and agrees as follows:

1. To proceed to Honolulu by the vessel provided for him in accordance with this Agreement;

2. On arrival at Honolulu to accept such employment as the employer may, under this contract, assign to him;

3. During the continuance of this contract being the full period of three years from the date, such employment actually begins to fulfill all the conditions of this Agreement, and to diligently and faithfully perform all lawful and proper labor and to obey all lawful commands of the employer, his agents or overseers, and to work during the night and rest during the day, if called upon to do so, and to work on all days which are not holidays and as such recognized by the Hawaiian Government, except when the said Laborer may be employed in domestic service, in which case the usual and indispensable work shall be done on these days also.

4. A day's labor shall mean to be 10 hours actual work in the fields, or 12 hours actual work at the Sugar factory, the hours not being continuous, but allowing the necessary time for taking food and rest. The hours of service are counted from the moment regularly established for the departure to the work in the factory or the fields, and the laborer must not exceed the time reasonabl necessary to arrive there. And 26 days actu work as aforesaid shall constitute one month's lab

Contract.

This Memorandum of Agreement made and entered into at Bremen this ___ day of *April* 1897, by and between *the Bremen Sugar* ___ of ___ **Hawaiian Islands,** of the first part, hereinafter called the employer, represented by **Carl Henoch** Jr. his duly qualified agent in Germany, and the laborer *Medicki Andric* now residing in *Cicakia* of the second part, hereinafter called the laborer.

Witnesseth that,

Whereas the said laborer is desirous of going to the Hawaiian Islands, there to be employed as an agricultural laborer, and in consideration of free steerage passage to the Hawaiian Islands to be furnished to him and his wife and 3 of his children by the employer, the following Contract has been concluded between the aforesaid parties to this agreement:

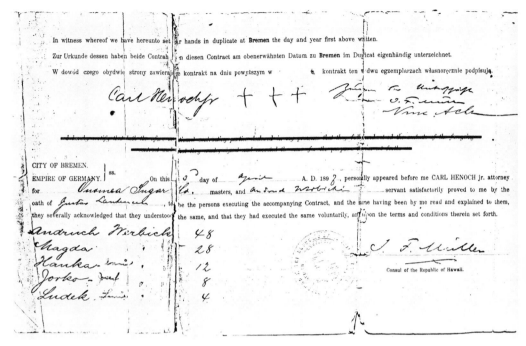

when he assigned innocent children into servitude.

For the next sequence of events and the eventual boarding of the vessel that was to transport the laborers to Hawaii, and their experiences enroute, we have to depend on the information provided by Rev. Ivan I. Ardan, editor of the Ukrainian paper "Svoboda". This information comes from a letter written to the editor by one, Dmytro Puchalsky, who at the time of writing had been in Hawaii for two years and was working on the plantation of Onomea in Papaikou in the district of Hilo of the Hawaiian Island.

> It was a German agent, F. Missler (sic!) of Bremen who convinced us to go to the Hawaiian Islands; he virtualy "smuggled" us out of the country. To forestall any detection, he drew us a map showing how we were to proceed to the Bremen port, ostensibly to safeguard us against apprehension, (more likely) from being detected by his competitor, Morowitz, who seemed to have an upper hand in selling steamship tickets to Canada or some other person who would give us a word of warning.[4]

Once the contract workers reached the seaport with their baggage, they were directed to proceed on board of a small luxury vessel. On board this vessel they received courteous treatment and before long it left the port. On board a fine reception awaited them: they were wined and dined, D. Puchalsky writes: "they gave us various drinks and plenty of food — all without charge,"[5] and as the emigrants were entertained royally their lux-

[4] Dmytro Puchalsky, L.S. to I.I. Ardan, editor, "Svoboda," Mt. Carmel, Pa. No. 19, 17 May, 1900.
[5] Ibid.

urious vessel sailed away from land into the open sea. After some six hours of sailing in the darkness of the night and in the North Sea fog, they rendez-voused with a bark that awaited them. Then they were directed to debark, "walk the gang plank" and go on board the sailboat. Once on board, they came to a rude awakening and realized that they were entrapped; and that they were deceived; that they were in serious difficulties.

The new vessel, it appears, was a sailboat, old and unclean. It was mann-ed by burly sailors and an equally disreputable looking captain who barked out orders in German, a language most of them knew. They were ordered to their accommodation below. It was unclean and uninviting.

True, the laborers travelling to Hawaii, saved the cost of the passage there, but paid for it otherwise — with miserable treatment. This, they discovered to their chagrin, the next morning after boarding the miserable bark.

In the morning the emigrants from Bremen faced the cruel reality of the voyage ahead — a voyage from which there was no chance of escape, or return; and which may be evaluated by the meals they received:

> In the morning we were given bitter black coffee and a litre of water. At noon we received half a litre of soup (at times less). In the evening we had black tea, without a pinch of sugar and a pound of zwieback. Such were our 24 hour ra-tions and sometimes we got less. This type of rations continued during our four month voyage.[6]

At last the deluded pilgrims on their way to a New Jerusalem were out on the Atlantic. The ship set course along the route travelled ninety-three years earlier by their Ukrainian precursor, Captain Urey Lisiansky.* Their heading was for Cape Horn.

A day out into the Atlantic saw no improvement in conditions or rations. The women, after feeding the children, very likely with their last crust of dried rye bread, no doubt, appealed to their husbands to ask the captain to provide more and better food rations, particularly for the children. These appeals fell on deaf ears.

*   *   *   *   *

When the German sailing vessel reached the equatorial area of the Atlan-tic and the winds became very calm and gentle — and near doldrum condi-tions set in, the captain gave orders that the "pilgrims" bring all their bag-gage on deck: their cases, duffle bags, and hand trunks and other bundles. If judged by what other settlers bound for Canada were bringing with them, we may assume that they carried clothing suggested by those who preced-ed them and utensils, hoping to establish themselves as farmers in a coun-try much colder than Hawaii. On deck they were ordered to open up their packing cases, hand trunks and duffle bags and instructed to separate from the rest of their contents a few light clothing suitable for summer wear. There is no doubt that the women were bringing some of their better clothing,

---

[6] D. Puchalsky, ibid.
* See Appendix I.

skirts, blouses, caftans, and white sheep-skin coats they had packed away and also bedsheets, their bedspreads, embroidered pillow cases, pillows and feather ticks. Generally in these items they wrapped their family icons, an earthenware bowl (makitra), a few cooking utensils, and also a grate (hruba) for their intended oven, "peech". Most women settlers also carried little bundles of vegetable and flower seeds. The men had tools, and other equipment. They brought tools needed for the building of homes and clearing of land: hatchets, broad axes, axes, mallets, hand-saws and their frames tied in neat bundles. Some had squares and compasses, planes and chisels to do finer work. Tradesmen brought their tools: the cobbler his awl and last; the bricklayer his trowel; and the musician brought his fiddle or cymbalons.

It is necessary to add that most of the letters also carried Bibles, hymn books and catechisms — the village clergyman who certified that they were people of good moral character insisted on these. Some included primers and other books which could be used to teach their children at home.

Once the travellers separated the things the captain ordered them to carry the few items below deck, the rest was hurled overboard by the sailors. The Hawaii bound laborers were, therefore, left denuded, and no doubt, the men cursed the captain and the women cried.

As the sailboat plied slowly southward toward the Horn, the disenchanted travellers, — one may well imagine — stood on deck in agony, distress and in fear of what the future held in store for them, as they watched their all sink into the equatorial waters of the Atlantic. Thus disappeared the few items they treasured and the tools and equipment with which they hoped to build the future wellbeing for themselves and their children — to start a new life in the "New Land", the promised land!

In the annals of history, it is likely that only Britons (in the days of Julius Caesar) being taken into the Roman bondage; the African slaves taken to the cotton fields of the "Deep South"; or in the more recent era, the famished Irish peasants or the Scottish crofters forced on board the barks for transportation to North America suffered greater agony, distress and humiliation than did the deluded group of Ukrainian pilgrims Hawaii bound in the summer of 1897.

*   *   *   *   *

The suffering of the group of innocent pilgrims began to intensify after the miserable bark crossed the equator and soon, in fact, conditions became unbearable.

Rounding Cape Horn

D. Puchalsky in writing about the part of the trip around the "Horn" states:

> And when they started to round that miserable "Caporee" (Cape Horn), possibilities for parting with this world were greater than ever reaching our destination. It was extremely cold — and since the warm clothing and bedclothes were cast into the sea — the people asked the captain to provide them with blankets and warm clothing, they also begged food and water. . .[7]

Though, as a general rule, the brutal, sadistic, treatment of travellers and sailors on board the ships by captains seemed to have been greatly reduced after the Captain Bligh episode, the German captain, in charge of the bark, even toward the end of the nineteenth century, it appears, continued with the primitive practice of flogging. The Ukrainian indentured laborers bound for Hawaii were unfortunate to be on board a ship where the captain had a beastly disposition for administering physical punishment and unfortunately it so happened that the people who left Western Ukraine despising the Hapsburg rule would have to sail with a German captain. They, it is understood, had to protect their women at all times and in retaliation he half-starved them and did not hesitate to flog the men if they complained:

> . . .The captain, the cursed German, said (to those complaining): "If you are not satisfied, then jump into the sea." And if, however, anyone pressed his request too persistently, the captain would order the sailors to bring the man to him, force him down, hold him flat on the deck; then he administered the punishment: ten to fifteen strokes with a wet rope. After that they would manacle the poor wretch and tie him to the mast where he was left for a period of two hours. Then when he was released from the mast the captain would strike him twice, once on each cheek, saying: "This is your breakfast!".[8]

Puchalsky's version of the inhumane treatment of the Ukrainian indentured workers by the German crew is verified by Polish sources which state that the laborers bound for the Hawaiian sugar plantations were treated on board the German vessel as slaves who on arrival in Hawaii were to be sold.[9] That was part of the reason, no doubt, why they received such wicked treatment from the German crew.

When the miserable German sloop rounded the Horn and left the Drake

---

[7] Puchalsky, D., ibid.

[8] Ibid.

[9] "The Great Migration": A document from the University of Ottawa School for Graduate Studies, p. 79.

Passage, it started to sail on less turbulent waters of the Pacific and then boredom set in — the people found it difficult to tolerate the tediousness of the voyage. It must be, therefore, recognized that they were people of strong mental fiber to withstand the horrors of the long voyage without many mental breakdowns.

The first group of contract workers from Western Ukraine, after a four-month sea voyage, arrived in Honolulu on the 27th of May, 1897. They made the voyage on the H.F. Glade with the "cursed captain" F. Haesloop as master. On their arrival they were unceremoniously placed into make-shift quarantine sheds where they remained for two days. Then, less ceremoniously they were driven into immigrant sheds, divided into small groups and taken to the various plantations, with the Ukrainian going mainly to the Hackfeld and Co. plantations — one on the Island of Oahu and the other on the Big Island at Papaikou.

A study of the passenger list[10] of the workers arriving on H.F. Glade shows that the Ukrainian laborers selected were young single men in the main. Their average age was 24 years and the age range was between 18 and 48 years — a fairly select labor force.

List of men to arrive in Hawaii on 27 July, 1897, as contract workers. Ages given in brackets: Chrapek, Toma (30); Dudek, W. (40), Durbazek, Wasyl (18), Dursky, Andrey (22); Guzelek, Iwan (19); Holowaty, Theodor (18), Holota, Michal (25); Konika, Iwan (32), Kochan, Toma (26), Kwaskowsky, Josef (27), Kozlowsky, J. (22), Dryla, Toma (24), Dranowsky, Michal (39); Lakusta, Mykola (20); Markievicz, Josef (26), Mularsky, Josef (26); Navikowsky, Pavel (23); Pawlowsky, Iwan (20), Puchalsky, Dmytro (23), Puchajsky, Ewan, (24); Sliwa, Michal (22), Slonski, T. (26), Sokolski, Michal (25), Suchylo, E. (22); Wasczuk, Mikolaj (25), Wacyk, Iwan (37), Wasilowsky, F. (22); Yakymishyn, Panko (47), Yakimishyn, Wasyl (20); Zolkowsky, J. (30).

The men in the older group were those who arrived with their families. The following is a list of seven family groups: Buchkowski — Josef (26), and his wife (20), Jasko (11/12); Mykola; Czorny (Chorney) — Theodor (38), Anna (37), Michal (14), Petro (10), Pawlo (5), Maria (3), Kaska (11/12); Florkiw — Josef (36), Magda (26), Hanka (12), Maria (7), Leon (5), Jaga (2); Hoculak — Tymko (30), Katryna (29), Demko (5); Holowatai (Holowaty) — Mykola (39), Anna (26), Sofia (4); Ruczarski — Iwan (48), Tekla (38), Josef (18), Nastia (20), Anna (6), Michal (11/12); Werbicki — Andrych (48), Magda (28), Hanka (12), Yurko (8), Ladek (4).

---

[10] Public Archives of Hawaii, Honolulu. (The names of villages from which they came were not given).

Office building in Onomea and road sign to Papaikou 1985.
—(M. Ewanchuk Coll.)

Onomea Bay c. 1900.

Chapter 3

Background of Contract Workers in Hawaii

When the first group of Ukrainians arrived in Hawaii, the practice of bringing contract laborers to work on sugar cane plantations was fairly well established. Therefore, in order to evaluate fully the experiences of the Ukrainian laborers, it appears necessary first to review the importation of other workers and to analyze the practices and conditions of work, which became well established during the last half of the nineteenth century.

In spite of the American protests about importation of indentured and coolie labor to Hawaii, the Hawaiian planters with the cooperation, tacit approval and assistance of their government continued to increase the contract labor force and develop their sugar industry, which it seems, accelerated in growth with the arrival of each new entrepreneur to the Islands. One of these men soon gained prominence, and through the years, played a vital part in the development of sugar cane cultivation and particularly in the importation of labor. He was Heinrich Hackfeld, who on coming to the Islands got first established as a merchant. In 1849 he opened a general store in Honolulu. His business operation was a great success and became the forerunner of the now "highly successful Liberty House chain of stores".[1]

Hackfeld, the former German sea captain and China trader, saw his business grow and soon became recognized for his business acumen and three large sugar cane plantations appointed him their agent. While Hackfeld was acting in the capacity of a business agent, he took every available opportunity to expand his enterprise and acquired ownership of large tracts of land most suitable for the growing of sugar cane; and began to manage "a vast sugar and real estate empire" in Hawaii. This is evident by the fact that by 1885, when he brought the first Japanese contract laborers to Hawaii, he had acquired the majority ownership in the Pioneer Mill Company.[2]

Chinese Labor

It appears, however, that the Chinese contract laborers were the first to be brought to Hawaii. This happened during the sandalwood era. In 1852, 195 debarked in Hawaii, 175 went to work as field workers and 20 as domestics. They all signed five-year contracts at a wage of three dollars a month in addition to a free passage from China, food and clothing. At the end of five years half of these returned to China driven out of the Islands by hard plantation life, flogging, gruelling toil on the sugar cane fields, and loneliness for wives and families. But in time more arrived and were subjected to much the same treatment and worked under similar conditions.

---

[1] A Brief History of Hawaii's Largest Company: AMFAC INC. p. 1.
[2] Ibid.

(At the present time, it is estimated, the Chinese population stands at about 56,000).

The Chinese laborers were reluctant field workers on plantations, and those who did not return to China, tended to gravitate into Hilo and Honolulu, where they started small businesses. Since the recruitment of the Chinese was not very selective — they were not medically screened — many with serious infectious diseases, and poor health in general, were admitted to the Islands. Such men, though willing workers, found it difficult to cope with the demands of the plantation lunas and many died, while others deserted.

The Coming of the Portuguese

Though some of the Portuguese seafaring men may have come to the Islands as early as 1790, the first permanent immigrants, 120 men, women, and children arrived on the German bark "Priscilla" in 1878.[3] They braved a 15,000 mile voyage over the turbulent oceans under the most primitive conditions of travel. Being driven from the Madieras by unemployment and hunger, they agreed to go to Hawaii provided the whole family could move. In the Islands they were fortunate to be able to receive spiritual guidance from the Roman Catholic clergy and soon were able to establish a viable nucleus of a Portuguese community. As more arrived, they, it seems, found adjustment to the Islands easier.

Scandinavian Labor

During the sandalwood and whaletrade periods many mariners began to come to the Hawaiian ports, some from as far as Norway, and the planters soon found out that there was a large pool of unemployed men in the Scandinavian countries, and turned their attention to that source.

It is regrettable that it was the brave Norse searovers who were responsible in bringing the Norwegian people into the Hawaiian bondage. The leader of the project was no other than Christian L'Orange who was born in Drammen, Norway and settled in Maui. He travelled to Norway in 1880 and returned with 613 Norwegians, 31 Swedes and four Danes. Since three Scandinavian groups were included, no doubt, there were a few Icelanders among them too, since they were experiencing economic stress in their country. Norse women and children were included in the first group of Vikings.

The voyage from Norway to Hawaii was long, tedious and exhausting. As a consequence 24 men died, but seven children were born en route. "Beta", the first ship to leave Drammen, arrived in Hawaii in February, 1881; the second ship, the "Musca" did not reach Hawaii until May. The Scandinavians were divided into two groups, the larger one staying in Maui and the second group was taken to the Big Island to the Hitchcock plantation in Papaikou.

---

[3] "Honolulu Star — Bulletin," Feb. 19, 1985, p. 7.

The Maui Group

It did not take long for trouble to develop in Maui. The Vikings, after the most demanding voyage, would not succumb to oppression:

> . . .trouble marked the labor experiment. Promises made to Norwegians were not kept. The contracts in Norwegian signed by all the immigrants promised food for all wives; those in English signed by the planters provided only for wives who worked. The contracts covered three years, during which the new laborers had to work 10 hours a day in the field or twelve hours in the mill, 26 days a month, for which men were paid $9.00 a month, a woman $4.50, together with board, lodging and medical care.[4]

> The Norwegians complained of harsh treatment by the foremen, unexpected deductions from wages and other violations of their agreements.[5]

Norwegians Take Strike Action

The unrest among the immigrant laborers, particularly those on the Big Island, finally led to a strike by the Norwegians against the Hitchcock Plantation — the first such strike in Hawaii's history. The men were jailed and, when the jail was full, others were sent to prison on other islands. After having received complaints, including letters and newspaper stories that likened the situation to "slavery", the Kings of Norway and Sweden appointed a diplomat representative, Anton Grip, who came to Hawaii to investigate. Many of the problems were resolved and the sugar planters corrected some of the situations which had led to unrest. Contract time was shortened, and pay and allowances were improved. But most of the Norwegians had already decided to leave the ranks of labor.[6]

It is necessary to observe, however, that the Vikings were not able to abrogate their contracts with ease. They had first to satisfy their obligation in paying for the cost of transportation to Hawaii.

Japanese Contract Laborers

The Japanese indentured laborers came to the Islands later than the Chinese. On February 8, 1885 the first group arrived. There were 100 of them. They were recruited by Robert Walker Irwin who received $5.00 in U.S. gold coin for each person shipped to Hawaii and a part of a $15.00 brokerage fee for each laborer.

The Japanese laborers were not as docile as the Chinese and trouble started almost immediately after they arrived. They found working conditions horrendous. In 1885 at Paia on Maui, five workers died from sickness and abuse, or a combination of both. . .In 1886 the workers at Koloa on Kauai charged that pay was irregular, that they were not allowed to cook, and that some were ordered to work when sick. When about 50 laborers refused to work,

---

[4] The Land of Aloha, by Keith Haugen, p. 90.
[5] Ibid.
[6] Ibid.

they were fined, and those unable to pay the fines were jailed.

The laborers that arrived from Japan came under an agreement whereby their steerage passage and food was provided; before leaving Japan, they were each advanced nine dollars. Employment was assured for three years and men were paid $9.00 a month and the women, if they wanted to work, $4.50.

> A working month consisted of 26 days, ten hours per day in the field and 12 hours in the mill or sugar house. Overtime pay was 12½ cents per hour.[7]

They like the Chinese endured intolerable hardships, and one, Kawasaki tells that:

> Every morning, the men would remind each other to bring along their rice bowls, which they wrapped in "furoshiki" (like a kerchief) and tied to their belts.

> At lunch, Chinese cooks doled out a single bowl of rice to each worker and a small piece of salted salmon or dried beef. If a worker forgot his bowl he would have to hunt for a banana leaf to serve as a plate, Kawasaki told his son-in-law.

> Raincoats at $2 each were too expensive for laborers who earned about $9.00 for 26 days of work, said Goto. Instead they would tie "goza" or straw mats to their backs. That didn't give the laborers much protection in a downpour and Kawasaki said the workers would get drenched and look like "wet rats."[8]

The pattern, therefore, seemed to be established for other contract workers who were recruited for work in Hawaii.

The Japanese contract workers continued to be brought to Hawaii until 1894 when the last shipment of government-contract laborers arrived. It is estimated that since 1885, 26 ships had brought about 26,000 contract immigrants from Japan.

German Laborers

German laborers were among the earlier recruits from Europe. They were selected by the personal agents of H. Hackfeld and Company. The German administrators, however, would not likely subject their kinsfolk, "vervandshaft" to the same abuses and exploitations that the lunas* imposed on the other contract workers. They, too, were given a greater opportunity to remain in larger groups while the other workers were dispersed. This is verified by Eleanor C. Nordyke when she writes:

> German immigrants were selected by a private commercial firm, H. Hackfeld and Company, with more regard to their adaptability to semitropical climate and plantation work. Almost 1400 arrived from northwest Germany between

---

[7] Honolulu Star Bulletin, p.6, p.7.
[8] Ibid.
* overseers

1881 and 1897. Under the paternalistic care of a Kauai sugar plantation, they formed a successful community which continued their homeland customs.[9]

Nevertheless, 1400 was not a large number of recruits to arrive in Hawaii during the span of some twenty years. It would appear that though they received good treatment in Kauai, all those arriving in Hawaii, however, could not receive placement in Kauai, and when assigned to other plantations to work under lunas of non-Germanic ethnic group they were as maltreated as were the other Europeans and the Asiatic laborers. Consequently, letters received in Germany would tend to discourage great numbers from immigrating to Hawaii, though during the period thousands left for Brazil and the corn belt of the United States. It is also difficult to accept the assumption that the Germanic laborers adapted more readily to semitropical conditons. Adjustment, if any, was more likely due to favorable conditions of work and less harsh treatment, and once they were able to live in a community of their own people, their adjustment was much easer, "especially on plantations operated by their own people."[10]

Credit must be given to H. Hackfeld that he was not willing to bring too many of his own people to Hawaii and place them in bondage. Therefore, when the first Ukrainian group was recruited in 1897, the German laborers coming to Hawaii with that group were conspicuous by their absence. In 1898, there were not more than a dozen laborers with German names sailing to Hawaii on the H.F. Glade. Among them were: Ernst Rohde, his wife and a family of three. They were from Halberstadt: Carl Engler and family: Albert, Brendt, and Gustav Steinke, all from Hammerstein; Johann Meyer from Bavaria and Emilie Pooch and her two-year old daughter from Bremen. Her husband very likely preceded them and she was travelling to join him. This group, it would appear, was the tail-end of the 1400 German laborers who came to Hawaii, as contract workers.

The French in Hawaii

The French did not settle in Hawaii as immigrants, neither were they brought into the Islands as indentured laborers. After Captain Cook discovered the Islands, a French captain, Count de La Perouse remained briefly in Hawaii where he landed in Maui in May of 1786. The greatest involvement of the French in Hawaii, was in getting approval for the Roman Catholic clergy to be able to get established in the Islands as they were previously deported from Hawaii, evidently on the suggestion of the Protestant clergy. This, therefore, made it possible for Father Damien to make his great contribution and sacrifice.

It is difficult to understand why the planters did not have the grace and the foresight to change their attitude to "cheap labor". It is more difficult, too, to understand the training received and the methods employed by the

---

[9] Eleanor C. Nordyke, The People of Hawaii: Honolulu: University Press of Hawaii, 1977, pp. 32-33.

[10] Andrew W. Lind Hawaii's People, Honolulu: The University Press of Hawaii, 1955.

lunas. These "satraps", after all, were once themselves, in the same predicament or were the descendants of the Portuguese, Scandinavian, French and German indentured laborers who were exploited and abused; one would think that they would show more understanding of the sufferings imposed on the new recruits. And as far as the planters were concerned, they did not seem to profit from past experience: they continued to treat their labor unfairly and were from year to year having to get a fresh supply. By 1900, they knew that their supply of European labor was nearly cut-off and they did receive a warning from the American leaders.

Free plantation house to live in — as advertised.

The living quarters for the families of Japanese workers on the island of Hawaii were simple thatched huts. *R. J. Baker Collection, Bernice P. Bishop Museum.*

Chapter 4

Further Recruitment of Ukrainian Laborers

After the arrival of the first group of 1897, and in spite of the difficult voyage, the group showed very good adjustment to the cutting and cultivating of sugar cane on the plantations. In the meantime the "H.F. Glade" was on its way back to Europe. F. Hackfeld and Company, soon wired instruction to Europe asking for another and larger contingent of contract laborers from Western Ukraine who could be contacted in the port cities as they were making arrangements to depart for "America". And it so happened that the people in Chortkiw area of the Ukraine had by this time received letters from their compatriots before they left Bremen for Hawaii, informing them and their relatives and neighbors about the very favorable contracts they signed to work on the islands that were described as virtual "paradise". These letters were added inducement to the information received in the villages from Missler as we learn from Pawlowsky's letter:

> When I was still in the Old Country in the village of Sokal, people used to come to me with letters they had received from Missler, and they would ask me for advice. The letters promised golden mountains in the far islands, and free transportation to reach them! (Translation)

Consequently, it was much easier to recruit laborers from villages where Missler had established contact, and from which the laborers of the 1897 group had already left for the Pacific Islands.

While the "Glade" was on its way to Europe around the Horn, H.F. Hackfeld and Company wrote a letter to the Hawaiian Minister of Foreign affairs to make arrangements for more Ukrainian laborers.

October 26, 1897

Henry E. Cooper, Esq.,
   Minister of Foreign Affairs
    Honolulu, H.I.
Sir:
   We have the honor to inform you that we have instructed Messrs, J.C. Pflueger & Co., Bremen, to recruit a further number of 194 European contract laborers to be sent here by sailing vessel for various plantations represented by C. Brewer & Co., Ltd., Wm. G. Irwin & Co., Ltd., and ourselves.
   43 laborers for C. Brewer & Co. Ltd.,
   25 laborers for Wm. G. Irwin & Co. Ltd.,
   126 laborers for H. Hackfeld & Co., total 194 laborers.
   to be accompanied by from 25% to 40% women and a number of children.
   These laborers are to be brought here under the present arrangement with the Hawaiian government, under which 10% of the number of Asiatic laborers

---

[1] Pawlosky from Hawaii to *Svoboda*, May 11, 1899.

imported shall be brought here in European and American laborers, and under
which the Hawaiian government has agreed to pay the cost of passage of the
women and children not to exceed $130.00 per family.
    We have the honor to be, Sir,

                                              Your obedient servants,
                                              (signed) H. Hackfeld & Co.

In October, 1897 the Minister of Foreign Affairs received another letter
from H. Hackfeld and Company, acting as the chief recruiting agent for some
of the Hawaiian planters, dealing with the families of the Ukrainian workers
who did not sail with the first group. It is not clear whether those families
were returned to their native villages from Bremen or that, in their case,
the recruitment was done in the villages and the wives were told they could
not accompany their husbands to Hawaii. The letter also created an impression that the contract workers of 1897 were very satisfied with their contracts and working conditions. In part it reads:

> Sir,
>   We are informed by the manager of the Lihue Plantation Co. that five of the
> laborers, who recently arrived here on board of the German ship "H.F. Glade"
> under contract to the Lihue Plantation Co., have left their wives behind, having
> through some misunderstanding been told that their wives could not go along
> with them. These people are very anxious to have their wives come out with
> the next expedition of emigrants from Bremen to this port, provided the Hawaiian
> government will under the circumstances be prepared to pay the cost of the
> passage of the wives and children (if any), not exceeding the sum of $130.00
> — for each family.
>   We most respectfully beg to submit this matter to your kind consideration,
> and hope that the Hawaiian government will assist these laborers to have their
> families join them. We beg to add that the percentage of women among the
> immigrants who arrived here per "H.F. Glade" amounted only to a little less
> than 25%.[2]

However, when the families arrived the Minister of Foreign Affairs received an unanticipated surprise: The German transportation company bringing the families to Hawaii — and only three not five — had seen fit to charge
more for this small group of people. Therefore, Hackfeld and Company had
to ask the minister, Henry E. Cooper, for an additional sum to cover the cost:

> In reply to your esteem favor of today, we beg to say that the actual cost of
> importation of the three families we (booked with) J.C. Pflueger, has exceeded
> in each case the sum of $130.00
>
> For your guidance we beg to say that the following amounts have been paid
> by us for account of the following plantations:
>   Lihue* Plantation Co.   1 woman 4 children $288
>   Kikaha Sugar Co.   1 woman 2 children $192
>   Meier and Kruse   1 woman 1 child $144[3]

[2] Hackfeld and Company to Henry E. Cooper, Oct. 28, 1897.
* In Kauai
[3] Hackfeld to Cooper, Honolulu, Oct. 28, 1897.

As a consequence of the increased cost of transportation per person, the Hawaiian government limited the amount which it was prepared to pay to $130.00 and the number of family groups to 30%. Hackfeld and Co., nevertheless, informed the government that 40% of the incoming laborers could be family groups.[4]

Since messrs, J.C. Pflueger and Co., were recruiting European laborers for the second group, it appears that the company experienced some difficulty in getting the required number. This is evidenced by the fact that only three of the five wives left behind agreed to come and that the number of family groups had to be increased to 40% as it was difficult to get the requested quota. Hackfeld and Co., therefore, had to request the Government to extend the bonds for the number of laborers ordered. The bonds were issued for laborers as follows:

Oahu Sugar Co., actually Hackfeld and Co., 100* men: Pioneer Mill Co., 17 men: C. Brewer and Co., 43 men: Wm. G. Irwin and Co., 25 men: the rest were ordered by four other companies.[5]

By 1897 the Hackfeld enterprise in Hawaii was well-established in Honolulu and continued to carry out the functions of a recruiting agency for the "Planters' Association". By this time it had attained a very formidable business status and operated from a fine building on the corner of Fort and Queen's Streets, in Honolulu. That year the "Paradise of the Pacific", p. 11, reported on the operations and listed the executive of the company:

H. Hackfeld & Co., is the principal commission house in the Pacific. It is the agency of the largest mail steamers that cross this ocean and furnishes supplies and sells the sugar of some of the most productive plantations of these Islands. It also controls an extensive coffee and fertilizing interest. In its merchandising department it ranks first in Honolulu. Its officers are: John F. Hackfeld, President; F.W. Klebahn, Secretary; H.P.F. Schultze, Treasurer; W. Pfotenhauer, F. Klamp, and George Rodiek, Directors; and John F. Humburg, Manager of the San Francisco branch.

It seems that one may conclude that the H.F. Hackfeld Co. had the controlling interest in the vessel "H.F. Glade" and was also in partnership with the Pflueger enterprise.

The Second Group Hawaii Bound

In the summer of 1898, another group, and larger than the one to arrive in 1897, set sail for Hawaii — and on the same ship, the "H.F. Glade." Unknown to them the lot of the first group in Hawaii was as miserable as

---

[4] Hackfeld to Cooper, Honolulu, Nov. 8, 1897.

[5] Ibid.

** Actually according to Hackfeld's letter to Cooper of Oct. 26, 1897, 126 men were ordered for the Hackfeld plantations.

Mill workers at Hutchinson Plantation, Standing 2nd from right: Heinrich Isenberg.
(On the far right, the huge man was likely the luna.) c. 1905 (Bishop Museum).

the four-month journey. From the day the contract laborers landed, they
began to press for the abrogation of the contracts. By the time the second
group arrived, the first group had had a fill of being harried at work to the
point of exhaustion, beatings and fines. They lived under excessive restraints,
and were denied the right to go to the nearest urban centres, particularly
those working on the Hackfeld plantation close to Honolulu. This restric-
tion became forcefully put into effect just before the arrival of the second
group. This, however, was a well-calculated action. Its object being to prevent the new arrivals from being informed about the deplorable working
conditions, and high cost of living, and the denial of elementary civic rights.

To get a better appreciation about the voyage of the second group to
Hawaii, we have to depend on specific recorded evidence — the interview
W. Chumer had with Mrs. Derko, nee Marusia Kucy, who as a young girl
came to Alberta from Hawaii after her father "worked out" his five-year contract. Mrs. Derko provides us with the following information:

> I was a little girl when I left with my parents for the Hawaiian Islands. When
> we left our village, our intention was to go to Canada or the Argentine. In Ham-
> burg, however, my father and some other people were persuaded to go to Hawaii
> for people were paid well there, they said, working on the plantations. Work
> was also available for women and children. Others signed to go there and so
> did my father...

> Each head of the family signed a five-year contract, otherwise he could not go
> there[6]...(translation)

---

[6] William A. Czumer, *Reminiscenses About Life of the First Settlers in Canada.* (Spomyny pro
perezhyvania pershych Ukrainskyh peresylentsivv Kanadu) Edmonton, 1942, pp. 29-30.

According to the available passenger list,[7] Mrs. Derko came to Hawaii with her family, Mr. and Mrs. Dominek Kucy, on October 6, 1898. The Kucy came from the village of Romashiwka in the District of Chortkiw, Western Ukraine — then under the domination of Austria-Hungary. The family consisted of the following members: Mr. Kucy, age 38; Mrs. Tacyjana Kucy 30; Pawlo, 14; Handzia, 12; Marusia, 7; and Ksenia, 4. The Koncohrad family and Demian Kindiak all arrived in Hawaii at the same time. All of these people were from the same village.

About half of the contract workers to come on the "Glade" in 1898 were destined for one of the two Hackfeld plantations, either the one connected with the Oahu Sugar Co., near Honolulu or the second one at Papaikou near Hilo.

From the Chumer interview with Mrs. Derko we get the following information about the voyage to Hawaii:

> I seem to remember that more than 200 people including children signed contracts; and when our boat left, there appeared to be some two thousand people on it. We travelled all the way by boat.

> ...and this took longer than six weeks — the journey became very tedious. Often the women cried saying that they were being taken to the end of the world.[8]

It is difficult to understand why Mrs. Derko made mention that they left from the port of Hamburg,* as the passenger list indicates that the Kutseys left Europe from Bremen. Her assertion that the number of Ukrainians travelling was 200 may be questioned as the passenger list recorded more. However, she was only seven years old and, therefore, could not be expected to have specific information.

There is no doubt that many of the passengers to disembark along the way were European settlers going to Argentine and Brazil; and many of them were emigrants from Germany; and also Czecks, Poles and Ukrainians.

Mrs. Derko did not report of any brutality during the trip, and this may have been due to the fact that after the arrival of the 1897 group in Hawaii, and the complaints made by these contract workers, Hackfeld and Co., could have instructed their German captain, Haesloop, of the "H.F. Glade" to desist from his former practices.

The route to Hawaii was the same followed by the D. Puchalsky contingent. Whether the people in the contingent, Hawaii bound on the "H.F. Glade", were asked to divest themselves of their tools and warm clothing they were bringing to Canada, is not known. However, since the Kutseys, when they finally arrived in Canada, had not a stitch of warm clothing, nor the Olaa forest settlers, it may be concluded that, they, too were ordered to give up their tools and warm clothing, and these were cast into the ocean.

---

[7] Hawaiian State Archives, Honolulu.

[8] Op. Cit.

* Unless the emigrants arrived in Hamburg and then were taken to Bremen, the "H.F. Glade" actually left from Bremerhaven.

Map of Ukraine

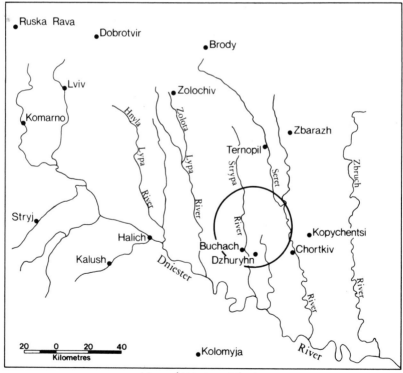

Map of Western Ukraine

Their travel was long and demanding and once they rounded the Horn and started to sail on the more peaceful Pacific, tediousness and monotony of the voyage seemed to set in and seemed to drive the women to distraction and despair — they feared the unknown — and as one started to cry the others joined her. Those who know the psychology of the Ukrainian peasant women would agree that they would actually ululate — wail bitterly and bemoan their fate:

> Mother of God, where are they taking us? Will they take us to the end of the world? Oh, my dear Mother, why did you let me go? Why did you let me take my children, my angels into the far-unknown from our Native Land? Now we are so far away: we will never return...they will take us to the end of the World and there plunge us into the void. Oh, Dear Lord, save our souls!

Such crying and wailing, no doubt, was part of the daily occurrence on the Pacific until they reached the end of their journey. The men, one may assume, were able to cope better with the stressful situation; and the children must have been bewildered and confused. Yet for them it was a great adventure.

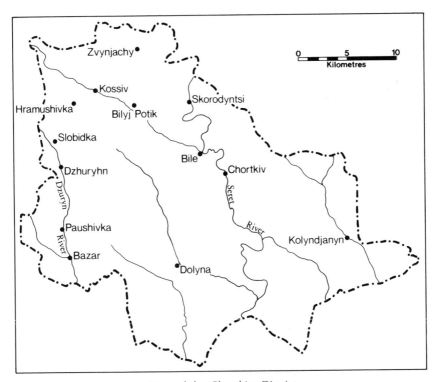

Map of the Chortkiw District
(showing location of some of the villages)

The following is a partial list of the villages from which the majority of the contract workers of 1898[9] came:

Bileypotik	Lviv (Lemberg)
Bilobozhnytsia	Monasterets
Brychkiwtsi	Novosadets
Buchach	Novosanch
Bukowa	Panchiwka
Dyzhnitsja	Romazhiwka
Dzhuryn	Sikuryntsi
Hrynkiwtsi	Slobidka
Kotsubychyky	Tryncha
Kossiw	Zvyniach

When the second group reached Honolulu, in spite of the travails at sea, the immigrants were impressed with the "New Land" and thought that indeed they had reached the "Promised Land", the "New Jerusalem", as they were informed by the recruiting agents that they would. It was a land of verdure, beautiful blue skies and gentle breezes. They looked forward to disembarking, selecting homesteads — as promised — establishing their families and then going to work.

However, once in Honolulu, like the first group, they remained in quarantine for a couple of days, received a very superficial physical examination and then were moved to sheds where representatives of the planters came and started to separate them into smaller groups.

The agents carrying out the distribution of laborers to various plantations appeared to have been very apprehensive: some interpreters sailing with the group from Europe, informed them that there were "ring-leaders", among the laborers, organizing them and making plans to attain the cancellation of the contracts which they signed because the recruiting agents misrepresented conditions.

In addition to misrepresentations the "Derko group" of laborers signed contracts that were far more demanding than those of the 1897 group; they bonded the laborers to the authority of the planter for a five-year term — longer by two years than the Puchalsky group contracts and carrying no provision for any adjustments in wages should economic conditions warrant such adjustment. Mrs. Derko informed that:

> ...There, in Honolulu, the people were divided into smaller groups and sent in various directions to work.[10]

However, Mrs. Derko does not seem to report to what island her parents were sent. Since she mentioned the Portuguese group, it would appear that they were in Oahu, close to Pearl Harbor where there was a concentration of Portuguese and Spanish workers, who later acquired land in that vicinity. Others were sent to Maui, Kauai, Molokai, and Hawaii. This dispersal of the large Ukrainian contingent immediately showed them that they had indeed reached veritable "Hades".

---

[9] Passenger List, Hawaii State Archives.
[10] Ibid.

PASSENGER

TO BE FILLED OUT AND SIGNED BY THE MASTER

Port of _Honolulu_

Name of Vessel _Ship "N. F. Glade"_ Name of Agent or Consignee _N_

Name of Master _Haesloop_ Port of Departure _Bremen_

NAME OF PASSENGER IN FULL	SEX	AGE years	PLACE OF BIRTH	OF WHAT COUNTRY A CITIZEN	LAST PLACE OF
Josef Bukawski	male	26	*	Austria-Hungary	
Mrs Bukawski	female	20	"	"	"
Mykola Bukawski	male	20	"	"	"
Jacko Bukawski	"	"/12	"	"	"
Jan Konika	"	32	"	"	"
Josef Mulawsky	"	26	"	"	"
Tomasa Chrapek	"	30	"	"	"
Franciscek Klinnick	"	40	"	"	"
Agnas Wallailin	"	20	"	"	"
Josef Shankis	"	33	"	"	"
Jurgis Bruno	"	39	"	"	"
Mikola Laverisan	"	18	"	"	"
Iwan Puchajsky	"	28	"	"	"
Jno Zoltowsky	"	30	"	"	"
Franciskus Alges	"	25	"	"	"
Frantisek Wasielwsky	"	22	"	"	"
Tomas Kochan	"	26	"	"	"
Andrzy Sursky	"	22	"	"	"
Josef Karaskawsky	"	27	"	"	"
Pavel Novikowsky	"	23	"	"	"
Jonas Koslawsky	"	22	"	"	"
Magda Pruss	female	42	"	"	"
Michel Pruss	male	18	"	23 "	"

With the coming of the second group of five-year contract workers to Hawaii, the number of Ukrainians to accept Hawaiian servitude increased, but others were on the way. It is difficult, however, to arrive at a precise number of Ukrainians, and for that matter, the number of other immigrants to come to Hawaii from Central Europe.

The Number of Ukrainians to Arrive In Hawaii

It is not possible to determine accurately the number of Ukrainian people who arrived in Hawaii during the period of 1897-1900. The figure most often

* See Appendix I: Western Ukraine

quoted is 350. In this figure are included the 37 families that D. Puchalsky reported arrived in 1897. However, in studying the passenger list of the H.F. Glade of 1897, it appears that he may have been referring to the number of single men only, who were later incarcerated in the Reef Prison. The total number on the first voyage to remain in Oahu was about 65. However, since the names of Bencharski and others that were on the first voyage do not appear on the passenger list, yet Bencharski worked in Papaikou in 1897, his calculations may deal with the Oahu group only and does not include the Halowatys, Hoculaks, Yakimishyns and Werbickis.

We know, however, that in 1898[11] on the second voyage of the "H.F. Glade" there were 46 women, 92 children, and 227 men, or a total of 365. This would bring the total number of immigrants to 420. But in addition to these, a very small number arrived on the S.S. Pfleuger[12] on December 10, 1898; and according to Theodore Luciw, they were the following: Wojciek Kuczek, 25; Kasimir Kudzak, 24; Szymko Pundyk, 30; Anna Pundyk, 24; Iwan Pundyk, 5; and Karolka Pundyk, 4. The Pundyk family was from the village of Slobidka and some of the Pundyk relatives arrived earlier. D. Puchalsky also reported that there were others who arrived on September 12, 1899.[13]

Though the first two groups followed the tedious one-third of a year voyage around the Horn, others did not do so. Julian Bachynski wrote:

> ...the immigrants who came to Hawaii later did not follow the Cape Horn route, but were transported by boat to New York, then by train to San Francisco, and from there they sailed to Hawaii.[14]

It is therefore, safe to estimate that the total number to arrive was close to six hundred.

Further Search for Labor

After the protests, strikes, and investigations engendered by the Central European laborers and the criticisms in the press, the planters of Hawaii brought the importation of Ukrainian and other Slavic laborers to an abrupt end. However, since there was a subsidy of $50,000.00 still available from the Hawaiian Government for the recruitment of labor, "other than Asiatic", the "Hawaiian Sugar Planters Association" in November of 1898, decided to take steps to utilize the available financial authorization and bring in other European laborers and, consequently:

> Meeting of November 5th was called to consider a proposition of the sugar planters for the introduction of Portuguese laborers as proposed under certain forms and conditions. An agreement with a form of contract attached was

---

[11] Report of Inspector of Immigration, p. 10.

[12] L.S. by Theodore Luciw of Minneapolis Minn., to Mrs. W. Lizak (nee Werbicki) of Mountain View, H.I., February 2, 1967.

[13] Puchalsky, op. cit. (passenger list for this group was not found in Honolulu).

[14] Bachynsky, op. cit., p. 183.

presented to the Board and approved, but upon conditions that the parties ordering these Portuguese laborers should enter into an undertaking with the Government to idemnify and hold harmless the Government from any pecuniary liability in the premises, either for passage money, or wages for the fulfilment of the contract.[15]

Once permission was granted, the sequences of events unfolded as follows: on the 9th of November a commission was forwarded to Mr. Hoffnang of London, a special agent of the Board of Immigration, to recruit Portuguese immigrants with the requisite authority to appoint sub-agents, one each at Azores and Madeira respectively.[16]

The decision to recruit Portuguese laborers was justifiable, if for no other reason than by virtue of the fact that there was a sizeable colony of their countrymen in the Islands. In 1898 Rev. Nestor Dmytriw[17] estimated the number of Portuguese in Hawaii at 15,000. Climatewise, too, it was assumed that these new immigrants would find adjustment to life on the Islands much easier.

On September 13, 1899 the "S.S. Victoria" arrived with the following Portuguese and Spanish laborers: 197 men, 57 women, and 83 children.[18] The "S.S. Victoria" contingent, however, was far short of the number anticipated.

> Over 800 Portuguese people were expected on the later steamer, but owing to misrepresentations by Thos. C. Jones, U.S. Consul at Madeira regarding the islands and our labor laws, it will be seen that only about two hundred and fifty came.[19]

> The misrepresentations consisted of notices being issued by the Mayor of Funchal, posted in conspicuous places and read in churches to the effect that the Government of the Hawaiian Islands did not favor the Portuguese immigration; that it did not recognize the validity of any contract which may be made by agents of Emigration of Immigrants, etc. The consequence was that some immigrants who had already gone on board deserted, and others booked, refused to embark.[20]

The failure to get the full complement of laborers from the Azores and Madeira was followed by the collapse of a scheme to recruit European laborers from Tyrol.

A group of Tyrolese who arrived by train from New York were, before boarding the boat for Hawaii in San Francisco, informed about the unsatisfactory conditions of life and work of the laborers in Hawaii. This led to desertion of 11 out of a party of 33 Tyrolese. "The Independent" blamed this situation on the press, the Ukrainians, and other laborers, who on buying their contracts and reaching the Mainland discouraged others from going to Hawaii. The "Independent" complained:

---

[15] Report of the Board of Immigration—Public Archives of Hawaii P. 10.

[16] Ibid. p. 10.

[17] N. Dmytriw, "Honolulu", "Svoboda", Feb. 1898.

[18] Op. cit., p. 10.

[19] Report of Hawaiian Immigration Agent, 1898-99, p.p. 12-13.

[20] Ibid.

These people were told in San Francisco that they were coming here to be enslaved. Some newspapers made a great outcry about it. There was no ground whatever for their scare, which was the work of cranks and "yellow journalists." It is of a piece with the base unprincipled row last year about the "Ukrainians" who had never been so well off before in their lives.[21]

On reading the testimonies in Dr. Peterson's report, one wonders how "The Friend" itself, had the audacity to defend labor conditions in Hawaii, and leads one to class its concluding statement in a special category of journalism. "The Friend" wrote:

The conditions of laborers in Hawaii is under government inspection and substantially good. "The Friend" seems called upon for this testimony on too well known matters of fact.[22]

The Ukrainian laborers must be given credit for precipitating a situation that caused an investigation. As a consequence, action for improvement was taken on some plantations. Dr. Peterson writes:

Following the series of inspections...there has been inaugurated, as a result, in many places a regular system of cleansing, not spasmodic but at short intervals. Camps have been moved to more favorable conditions. New camps have been built, old ones renovated and thinned out. Bath-houses, wash-houses, and kitchens have been built. Water from pure sources has been laid in pipelines, drains arranged and more or less satisfactory systems of closets prepared. *The treatment of the laborers has been brought nearer to legal status.*[23] (Italics those of the author).

Since the government of Hawaii did not include single women in its group of immigrants, along with the single men, its contention that it wanted settlers can only be interpreted as a misrepresentation; and, therefore, Thos. C. Jones, the U.S. Consul was justified in warning the Portuguese officials in Madeira and Azores, that settlers were not wanted.

By the end of 1899, all importation of European laborers to Hawaii under contract, therefore, seemed to end.

---

[21] "The Friend", Volume 38, No. 5.

[22] "The Friend", Volume 38, No. 5.

[23] Dr. Peterson's Report, p. 51.

Chapter 5

Negative Factors of Employment in Hawaii

The newly arrived contract workers who were sent from Oahu to other Hawaiian islands were actually fortunate to be farther removed from Honolulu, where the bubonic plague made its appearance; and as a consequence, there were many people ill and some died. On learning about the pestilence, the Ukrainian laborers were no doubt, struck with terror. They well remembered being told about the havoc the plague — brought in from Asia Minor — engendered in their native land.

The Honolulu Bubonic Plague

The bubonic plague which invaded Hawaii was most severe in Honolulu. The mortality rate, as reported by "The Friend",[1], was 112. Of this number 47 per cent were Hawaiian, and 34 per cent were Asians. The plague also spread to other islands; there were nine deaths in Maui. Of the cases in Honolulu, 35 were Chinese; 13 Japanese; 15 Hawaiian; 7 Whites; and one South Sea Islander. Of the total number attacked by the plague only 10 recovered. The number of Chinese to die was much higher than that of the other groups. The seriousness of the pestilence may be judged by the fact that the bubonic plague that invaded Hawaii was much more severe in Honolulu than in Alexandria, Egypt, a city ten times the size of Honolulu, where that same year the pestilence lasted six months with only 90 reported cases. Sanitation in Honolulu in 1897-1899, was, it would appear, of the lowest standard.

Another negative factor that greeted the European laborers was drought. It lasted from October, 1898 to April, 1899. "The Friend" also reported that during that period, there was, on the average, of only 1.62 inches of rain a month. Such a serious winter drought was never before recorded in the Islands. Consequently, serious problems arose in various areas as reported in the press:

> Several Chinese, at Manoa, got into a serious fight over the question of "water rights", one man's head being seriously cut with a mattock.

> A committee of stockholders and directors left for Molokai to investigate the water question and other conditions of the American Sugar Company.[2]

The group of Ukrainians, however, that was sent to the island of Molokai must have been most disturbed, no doubt, not only by the drought, but also having to bring their children so close to the island where the leper colony

---

[1] "The Friend", Volume 58, No. 5, p. 37.
[2] Ibid.

Fr. Damien, Martyr of Molokai: Statue in Honolulu, Hi. (M.E. Coll. 1985).

was established and where Fr. Damien met his sacrificial end. In time, they learned, how leprosy was brought to the islands by the Chinese and how those infected with the dreaded disease were sent to the part of the island surrounded by cliffs, and from which there was no return. The first "inmates" were brought there by ship from Honolulu and forced to swim from the ship to the shore. Their food supply was also dumped in a like manner and they had to swim out to sea to get it. The unfortunate people were given only 11 months to live — and died like flies. It is little wonder that the European laborers shunned away from the Chinese laborers, fearing that by close contact they ran the risk of contacting the Asiatic maladies.

Those who went to the Big Island also had their apprehensions; the Hilo harbor frightened them, particularly when they learned about the high tides. In its 100 year history, Hilo had suffered nearly 30 destructive tidal waves — some were "killer waves", killing people and destroying buildings and ships in the harbor. Then farther inland there were the two active volcanoes, Mauna Loa and Kilauea whose molten lava, when they erupted, flowed down the slopes in burning rivers. These factors — freaks of nature — made people fearful of their recurrence and thus made the beautiful island less attractive for permanent settlement.

A special dispatch from Seattle Washington, July 24, 1899 printed by "The Examiner" reported:

Hilo in Danger of Being Wiped Out by Molten Lava

The town of Hilo, which is threathened with destruction by a fiery stream of lava from Mauna Loa, is the second city in the Hawaiian islands. It is situated on Waiakea bay, and has a big and almost land-locked harbor. The city is a beautiful one, and is much frequented by tourists. Nearly all the output from the sugar plantations on the island of Hawaii is transported to Hilo, whence it is loaded on ships for the Pacific Coast.

Also in Hilo, then the king city of the sugar industry, the other repelling aspects were social segregation — few plantation workers lived in the city and could aspire to do so, but one could see rich entrepreneurs dressed in white and wearing Panama hats strutting with cane in hand along Hilo streets. These were the men of wealth and leisure who in receiving large grants of land became rich by exploiting coolie labor. Invariably in their promenades they were accompanied by parasoled ladies dressed in their best with their long skirts sweeping the sidewalks; and, as one writer remarked: oblivious to wearing petticoats with mouldy lace, as they were oblivious to the hardships endured by the laborers as a consequence of their exploitation. In this city of high humidity "a little mould" was accepted as something unavoidable; and laborers had to endure misery for they had signed contracts.

In Hilo, in addition to the "aristocracy" of that day, there also was an ample supply of "lunas", overseers, and drivers. This may be seen by examining a part of a page from the 1907 Directory of the Territory of the Island of Hawaii; under the letter "R". Among this group is listed the lone, known Ukrainian, Dr. Nicholas Russel (Suzdylowsky).

---

714   ISLAND OF HAWAII.

cano rd, Hilo.
Rowland Barney, lineman Hilo Elect Light Co, r Pitman, Hilo.
Rowland Mary Mrs, opr Hilo & Hawaii Tel & Tel Co, r Pitman, Hilo.
Roy E Mrs, land owner Kainaliu, p o Kealakekua.
Roy Wm F, live stock Kainaliu, p o Kealakekua.
Ruault C N Rev, pastor Catholic Mission, Waiohinu.
Rulia Carrie, r Ponahawai nr Pitman, Hilo.
Russell Nicholas, phys and cane planter Mountain View.
Rust David, luna Onomea Sugar Co, Papaikou.
Rust Joseph, luna Onomea Sugar Co, Papaikou.
Ryan E R, luna Hawn A Co, Pahala.
Ryan Thomas J, dep county treas, rms The Rainbow, Hilo.
Rycroft Mark A, timekpr Honomu Sugar Co, Honomu.

In the Orchid Island the Ukrainian laborers were not in one group, but found themselves scattered among different plantations — some of which were 12 and more miles from the nearest village — and they seldom visited Hilo. Work on the plantations required a strong back and powerful hands to wield the heavy, clumsy hoes, and the heavy mattocks used for the cutting of cane; and when the cane was cut and the leaves lopped off, they had to load the cane stalks on the wagons.

---

[3] H.R. 996, Huskd's Directory of Honolulu and the Territory of Hawaii, 1907, p. 7591. (Hawaii's Department of Education Library, Hilo.)

Location of Dr. N.K. Russel's home in 1907 and plantation in background.

Work on the sugar plantations, therefore, was most demanding, in fact it was veritable slavery in the true meaning of the word. People were hitched with horses to pull wagons loaded with sugar cane, and were whipped with cow whips like animals. There were ceertain specific restrictions, too: they were forbidden to leave the area where they worked. The daughters of indentured workers who wished to marry men outside the limits of the plantation had to pay $120 to the planter to be released.[4]

The laborers, consequently, began to complain. Their complaints reached the Inspector of Immigration who observed that: "Every country has the labor it deserves". He criticized the planters mildly pointing out that they could take better care of their labor: "The care of draught horses is as important as the fixing of the rate of pay;" and that, in like manner, the planters could provide better care for their labor, for it was claimed: ". . .the man who wields the hoe shall be handled with the least possible friction."

There is no doubt, however, that the planters took better care of their draught animals, that were their property, than they did of the "contract laborers". The planters, therefore, disregarded the Inspector's mild admonitions. But as complaints began to reach the authorities of the Territorial Government of Hawaii, Dr. Peterson, Inspector of Immigration, was requested to make a closer check on the situation. On making his preliminary

---

[4] Julian Bachynsky, p. 183.

report he expounded the unsatisfactory type of labor that was recruited for the Islands and deprecated the fact many labor groups did not try to apply themselves. He viewed these laborers with disgust:

> ...the slow intentional and lifelong laziness of many field groups, or the insolent loitering of a crowd taking an hour to a mile on the way to work...[5]

Nevertheless, he failed to condemn the planters for discouraging the workers by creating most unfavorable conditions of work and this led the laborers to resort to a type of "passive resistance". He, however, did observe obliquely: that those who want servile laborers and drive them contemptuously to menial and excessive work will prefer a class of laborers that will endure such conditions.[6]

Dr. Peterson, however, should have at that time addressed himself to the situation with more candor, and would have, no doubt, precluded much suffering.

Nowhere is there any evidence that the Ukrainian sugar cane workers did not apply themselves. They, it appears, were good workers and did not require a firm hand (with a cow whip) to urge them to do a good day's work; nevertheless, they objected to the long and demanding hours of work, and the punishment from the lunas. Seeing that pressure from the lunas did not abate, the laborers in Oahu took what they considered to be proper action. They appealed to the Austrian Consul in Honolulu, but receiving no assistance from his quarters, they took more drastic action:

> After a year of exhaustive work and humanly unbearable living conditions, the indenture (Ukrainian) laborers reached the limit of endurance and 37 workers in the district of Waipaha on the island of Oahu went on strike. . .(Hackfeld, the owner of the plantation) issued instructions that the strikers be arrested. . .[7]

By arresting the strikers, Herr Hackfeld was able to crush the strike action. It appears that the 37 arrested were single men, the married men, no doubt, did not dare go on strike and leave their families without support. The arrested men, however, were sent to do other work and were marched out of the prison each day by armed guards who supervised them at work.

The trouble of the planters did not end with the arrest of the thirty-seven:

> The news that the Ukrainian immigrants went on strike soon reached the Polish and the Latvian workers on the island of Maui, and they, too, went on strike — and were also placed under arrest.[8]

Soon on other plantations contract workers took strike action and some on the Big Island and Maui were imprisoned for disobedience.

Reverend Nestor Dmytriw, a Ukrainian Catholic missionary, who in

---

[5] Report of Bureau of Immigration, passim

[6] Ibid.

[7] Bachynsky, J., op. cit., p. 182.

[8] Ibid.

1897-98 for a brief period worked as Immigration Inspector in Canada and visited Ukrainian homesteaders (Sifton settlers) on their Manitoba farms, learned from these settlers that their relatives in Hawaii who worked on sugar cane plantations were treated like slaves. Such information was, no doubt, received by Peter Yakimishyn from his father in Papaikou, Hawaii who wrote to him in Ethelbert, Manitoba complaining about the difficulties the people were experiencing. Rev. Dmytriw, therefore, on his return to the United States, wrote an article in the Svoboda, entitled, "Honolulu". The intent of the article was to inform the Ukrainian immigrants planning to go to Hawaii to work about unsatisfactory conditions under which the "contract workers" labored, and to forestall further immigration to Hawaii. He made these observations:

> The owners of plantations, sugar refineries, cotton fields, and others have a right to hire contract workers. Which means that a laborer signs a three-year contract to work at a specific wage and cannot leave this employment sooner than three years. According to newspaper reports, the present government plans to abolish this barbaric law. Thirty-four of our Ukrainian laborers signed such contracts and came to Hawaii. They are now at a place called Papaikou on the island of Hawaii. They are working very hard under the hot sun on sugar cane plantations. Everything they buy is very expensive. . .Here I am listing names of several of our countrymen on that plantation: Nicholas Holowaty, Theodore Chorniyj, Tymko Hoculak, Panko Yakimishyn, Iwan Bencharski, Stanley Kawchal, and Wasyl Yakimishyn.* If anyone wishes to write to them, he should address the letter thus: Mr. Nicholas Holowaty, Papaikou, Hawaiian Island.[9](Translation)

In time strikes and more labor troubles began to erupt among the "Asiatic" groups. We learn from "The Friend" of the 6th of April, 1898 that:

> Labor troubles were reported at Lahaina among the Japanese of both the Pioneer and the Olowalu plantations.

"The Planters' Association of Hawaii" consequently laid the blame for labor troubles at the feet of the Ukrainian laborers, concluding that the importation of these laborers "was far from being a success."

> No sooner had the men been shipped to the various plantations than they began to make trouble trying to get out of their contracts. The lot sent to Oahu Sugar Company positively refused to work, and being arrested and brought before the Court were committed to jail until such time as they were ready to return to work. After several months working on the roads the plantation cancelled their contracts and allowed them to go.* Investigation brought out the fact that while these people were on board the vessel during the voyage to Honolulu, plans were formed by two or three ring-leaders to avoid fulfillment of their con-

---

[9] Nestor Dmytriw, "Honolulu", "Svoboda", Oliphant, Penn., U.S.A., February, 1898.

* Rev. Nestor Dmytriw did not state that some of these men, like Panko Yakimishyn were married and his wife, Ewdocha, was with him in Hawaii.

* There is no evidence, however, that they were all let go, a few maybe — those that had the money to pay for their release, but not all.

tracts. Another lot at Lahaina, Maui, also gave considerable trouble necessitating the Board's Immigrant Inspector making a trip to investigate matters.[10]

At the same time, D. Puchalsky, one of the more informed men of the 1897 group, was working on the Onomea plantation on the Big Island, where several other indentured Ukrainian workers were employed. Though abused and exploited, the majority of the members of various work groups considered their horrendously miserable situation neither eluctable nor immutable: not having a governmental agency to whom they could appeal for help, they wrote to Karl Genik who was a leader of the first group of Oleskow settlers to locate on homesteads in Stuartburn, Manitoba in 1896. He was then living in Winnipeg, where he was employed as an interpreter. They requested assistance in the abrogation of their contracts, and about coming to Canada. On receiving requests from Holowaty from Hawaii, Karl Genik took the only action available to him: He contacted Rev. Honcharenko in Hayward, California, who in turn informed Rev. I.I. Ardan, editor of the Ukrainian paper "Svoboda", that though "Svoboda" had written articles dissuading more Ukrainians going to Hawaii, that those who were there needed immediate help to extricate them from their Hawaiian misery.

It cannot be construed that the Ukrainian laborers were the only ones to suffer from the abuse of the lunas (and the "constabulary and judiciary" working in concert with the planters); other laborers suffered equal or worse maltreatment.

There were claims in the press that the lunas on the Hawaiian plantations had established worse work conditions than those of the cotton planters in the "Deep South" prior to the American Civil War; their maltreatment of workers was not restricted to their abuse of the protesting Ukrainian workers; their treatment of the Asiatic labor was even more despicable. Of the 414 Japanese laborers employed by the Pacific Sugar Mill and the Honokea Sugar Company, in 1898, 79 males or 19 per cent deserted, and in addition to these 79 men there were 16 women, bringing the total to 23 per cent — six died. The average reporting sick each day was three per cent.

In 1899 there were 821 Japanese males and 98 females employed by the two companies mentioned; of this number 22 died, three per cent reported sick every day and a total of 132 males and 26 females, or 17 per cent deserted. On the Island of Kauai that same year the Kola Sugar Company employed 496 Japanese men and women, and 13 died, which would be 26 per thousand. The percentage of sick per day was 5 per cent, and 11 per cent deserted. In examining the table on "Mortality, Sickness and Desertions of Japanese Laborers" for 1898 and 1899, it appears that labor conditions on the Big Island were much worse than those on the Island of Kauai.[11] This may have been due to the fact that the Big Island was farther removed from the centre of government, and where the excesses of the planters were less in the public eye.

---

[10] Report of the Board of Immigration, Op. cit.
[11] Charles A. Peterson, M.D., Inspector of Immigration Report, p. 50.

Laborers' Reports from Hawaii

Both the 1897 and 1898 groups that left Ukraine for Hawaii, had a better knowledge of Canada than they did of the United States; and by this time some of them had kinfolk and people from nearby villages in Western Canada who, though they were experiencing problems of pioneer living, in no way were in a state of bondage, but were free men. The Hawaiians also knew that Kyrylo Genik who came out with the first group to Manitoba in 1896, was since employed as an immigration agent. Therefore, finding themselves in a most stressful situation, they, therefore, wrote letters asking for advice and assistance.

As a consequence of information received, Rev. Ardan, the editor of "Svoboda," wrote to the people working in Onomea and Papaikou on the Big Island, and sent them copies of the "Svoboda", asking them to inform him in more detail about their conditions of life and work. After receiving letters from Hawaii, he published some in his paper. The first one was from Iwan Pawlowsky.

The Pawlowsky Letter

Onomea, Hawaii
July 7, 1898

Esteemed Editor of "Svoboda":

You wrote to us inquiring how we were getting along here, and asked that we inform you about conditions. I am, therefore, responding to your questions.

Very little, if anything else, is grown here except sugar cane. There are many different trees, some bearing fruit, but they are not like the trees in the Western Ukraine, with one exception — the peach trees are the same. It is very hot here, that is, periodically, for as rain follows rain, there are cool periods, too. It is difficult to find a clear sunny day as it rains so often; but then the sun begins to shine. It is hot and humid and one gets dizzy; but this does not last long for after two or three hours it rains again.

For protection from the rain we wear raincoats, which cost $1.50 each, but these hardly last us a month as they tear readily. It is difficult to save money here for one needs many work clothes, which don't last long, as they are soon cut to shreds by the sugar cane.

We work cultivating and harvesting, hoeing and cutting sugar cane. There are such flumes by which we float the cane to the factory, where it is changed into sugar. The flumes are made of boards and are propped up by posts. The water flows through them and carries the cane stalks to the factory. We work a ten-hour shift a day in the fields and receive $18.00 a month — for we signed such contracts; and if it so happens that some work has to be finished sooner, we work for more than 10 hours, and for two hours of overtime work we receive 25¢. It's true that no one is taking advantage of us, everything is in our contracts: We have running water in the house, free fuel, house and medical services — and $18.00. But what of it? Of this money we barely receive a half for the cost of food and clothing is high: 25 kilos of flour costs $2.00; 50 kilos of rice $7.00; 25 kilos of potatoes $1.25; 5 pounds of sugar 25¢; one kilo of salt 5¢; and all cereals are 5¢ a pound: A good suit of clothes costs $23.00 or $24.00; work shoes $2.00; and dress shoes $3.00 — everything is very expensive.

Sugar cane field workers (Bishop Museum)

There are twelve of us single men here and seven are married couples. The married couples who have children barely earn enough to cover their cost of living and can't save a cent.

It was Missler who sent us here. We wrote to him and his reply was: "If we wanted to go to work, my advice would be: "Go to Honolulu," he wrote, "go where there is free transportation, but because you will travel free of charge, you will have to sign a three-year contract." And that's what we did.

We arrived here on the 27th day of July 1897 — we travelled by sea from Bremen for four months before we reached Honolulu. We remained in the port for two days and then were sent to various islands.

There were many of us who arrived in Honolulu, about 200 Ukrainians and Poles from Western Ukraine. They sent the people to various places, and I don't know where they are now. There is no winter here, but only rain and heat.

We have a clergyman here, but what of it? We do not understand him for he only speaks Portuguese. I shall write more the next time. And now, please send us some books and more newspapers, for the people here like reading the "Svoboda".

Wishing you good health,
Iwan Pawlowsky[12]

It is pathetic to read that the people isolated in Papaikou requested books and newspapers. After a year in Hawaii they had not mastered English, and the closest source of reading material was the "Svoboda" in the U.S.A. — a newspaper organized mainly by Ukrainian miners in Pennsylvania. Whether they received any books and newspapers from the Western Ukraine is not known. What books they were bringing with them were hurled into the Altantic on the command of the wicked captain.

Part of the D. Puchalsky Letter

Here our people are engaged cultivating the sugar cane, hoeing, etc. — but the groups are separated from each other, and some may be found on all the islands. They are paid $18.00 a month and receive free accommodation in the houses provided them on the plantations. They buy their provisions in the plantation stores — paying $1.50 for a bag of flour; $4.50 for a bag of potatoes; and $8.00-$10.00 for a bag of rice — everything is very expensive. Here one pays $6.00-$7.00 for 100 pounds of the lowest grade of sugar; and a pound of coffee costs 40¢.

We signed the contracts in Bremen and arrived in Honolulu on July 27, 1897. Others came here on September 12, 1899.

D. Puchalsky, who provided information about the rigors endured by the members of the first group during the voyage to Hawaii, also provides information about the penalties imposed on him, at Onomea, when he failed to report for work.

I, Dmytro Puchalsky, was fined twice: once, when I tried to escape and the police caught me. I was brought before a judge and the Hawaiian court imposed a fine of $5.00 and 15 days in jail. (Those were the instructions of the planter John Moir). My second penalty came during the Ukrainian Easter. On Easter

---

[12] "Svoboda", 7 July, 1898. (translated from Ukrainian)

Monday, May 1, 1899, I wasn't feeling well, so I did not report for work. The planter phoned the authorities asking that a policeman be sent out as one indentured laborer did not report for work. The policeman took me to jail. The next day I was brought to the court where I was sentenced to a $10.00 fine or a jail term of 20 days. This was entered on my contract — both fines were recorded. However, I wanted to be released of my contract of indenture, and was successful in doing so by paying $40.00[13]

The penalties for desertion and illness were excessively heavy — ten dollars for being absent one day!

That D. Puchalsky may have not been feeling well is understandable. It was Ukrainian Easter and on Easter Sunday the Ukrainian laborers very likely celebrated Chrystos Voskres, (Christ is Risen), under the palm trees in their traditional manner. They, no doubt, gathered early in the morning to greet the morning sun by singing their Resurrection Hymn: Chrystos Voskres iz mertvych, (Christ is risen from the dead. . .) — one of the hymns that tends to bring the highest degree of hope to the Ukrainian worshipper. After their "Hawaiian" Easter breakfast, they likely spent the rest of the day celebrating, and D. Puchalsky may have carried the celebration too far!

Dmytro Puchalsky was able to buy his freedom from the Hawaiian indenture; and so did many others who had money available. These "freed contract workers" almost immediately left for the Mainland, for San Francisco, where they became active in dissuading other European laborers who were making plans to leave for Hawaii, and those who were transported across the U.S.A. by train instead of being taken around the Horn.

Credit is due to the Ukrainian laborers that they, though scattered among the islands and different plantations, seemed to maintain inter-plantation contacts, and eventually succeeded in establishing contact with the Ukrainian and American press. The articles that appeared in the press and the actions of their countrymen in the U.S.A., in time, led to their release from contracts.

In spite of the strict supervision and daily roll calls, periodically some Ukrainian laborers deserted. Rev. I.I. Ardan writes in the "Svoboda":

At the present time four men are in jail for desertion, and for trying to get work in another plantation. Hawaii, however, consists of islands each surrounded by water, so one is not able to escape far. Therefore, our countrymen, when they were caught by the mounted policemen, were kicked like dogs, and beaten over the head, neck, and shoulders with ropes and then tied to a horse, and so made to walk for three days or the time it took to get them to jail.[14]

Iwan Pawlowsky's Second Letter

In spite of being separated and scattered in small groups among the different plantations and islands, the contract workers managed to maintain

---

[13] As reported by Jar. Chyz, "Ukrainian Immigrants in Hawaii," Scranton, Pa., National Will Almanac, 1926 p.p. 81-82. (Originally, Puchalsky to Ardan, "Svoboda", May 17, 1900. (translation)

[14] I.I. Ardan Op. Cit.

The prison on Prison Street in Lahaina, Maui where the contract workers were incarcerated.

contact. This may be seen from Iwan Pawlowsky's second letter. Besides making reference to his group on the Big Island, he also writes about the laborers in Maui and Oahu.

In order to give the reader a fuller appreciation of the situation that existed, we are quoting Pawlowsky's letter in full:

> Onomea, Hawaiian Islands
> 7 January, 1899
>
> I am writing to you on behalf of those people who are now languishing in jails. They did not want to work under the conditions imposed on them by the contracts; they wanted to be free agents in selecting their work. For their attitude they were first beaten and then imprisoned. Now fifty are in jail — 22 young men age 22, 20, and 18 years of age, however, were released from their contracts because they were considered to have been under age when they signed their contracts. There is no law in effect for the release of other laborers. This took place in Oahu on the same island where Honolulu is. The place (plantation) is called Waipahu. It is also on the Island of Oahu.
>
> On the island of Maui the contract laborers also refused to continue working since the planters did not pay them for all the days they worked. The people complained that they had worked a whole month and were paid only for a half. They were told: "You worked for 26 days and we will pay you for 13 days and there is nothing anybody can do about it!" When the people refused to go to work, the police were summoned and the people were imprisoned. The wives of the imprisoned men cried bitterly fearing of facing starvation as there was no one to earn money to support the family. Then the women went to the prison to ask for the release of their husbands and said to the authorities: "Feed us

all here since you have taken away our husbands who supported us and our children." The authorities, however, drove the women away and now the poor souls have to beg food from the Chinese and Japanese homes. The majority of these people have come from Russia. They are Latvians and Poles in the main. There were also some from our country from the villages of Slobidka, Dzhuryn, and Kossiw.

On the island where we are now, there is one plantation, Pahala, where they beat people mercilessly and impose fines. Two Mazurian boys ran away from that plantation into the countryside and nobody has been able to capture them yet.

In our Onomea plantation the people wanted to stay home on Christmas Day and celebrate, but the luna came around and threathened them with a fine of $5.00 each and chased them all to work. There are twenty-seven of us working on this plantation, but I have not the exact information about the other plantations.

This, in short, is the bitter fate of the laborers in the Hawaiian Islands.

Iwan Pawlowsky[15]

The Banyan Tree

When in the early thirties, the late Dr. Luke Myshuha was collecting information about the Ukrainian immigrants in the United States, he reported that in San Francisco he was told an interesting story about the Ukrainians in Hawaii. Whether the story can now be authenticated is uncertain, however, it appears plausible and is connected with the imprisoned Ukrainian contract workers in Lahaina.

Some twenty or more years earlier a banyan tree was planted in the backyard of the courthouse, but though it took firm root, it seemed to be somewhat misshapen. On finding out that among the prisoners in the Lahaina Prison, there were two very experienced orchardists, the warden had the

The famous banyan tree in the courthouse yard in Lahaina. (M.E. Coll.)

---

[15] L.S. by Iwan Pawlowsky to Rev. I.I. Ardan, editor of "Svoboda".

prison work crew uproot the tree, and then the orchardist took over the operations of planting a large well-shaped banyan tree in its place. The prisoners were directed to water the newly planted tree every day and it grew to its present size covering the whole backyard. This supposedly was one of the more visible contributions of the Ukrainian workers on the Island.

* * * * * *

Mykola Holowaty's Letter

Letters to and from Hawaii were slow in reaching their destination, it seems, but Mykola Holowaty did not write his until some six months after the Pawlowsky's second letter. It is interesting to note that there were a number of men in the Papaikou — Onomea group who were able to write in Ukrainian. Mykola Holowaty was one of those who remained permanently on the Island and raised a fairly large family. He died in Hawaii. No further correspondence from him to the "Svoboda" is on record.

11 May, 1899

News from Hawaiian Islands

Sometime in May of this year, I received two letters from our people in the Hawaiian Islands, inquiring whether it was possible for them to be accepted as members of the "Ukrainian" National Association. I answered their query and requested that they send me additional information about our people in those Islands. As a consequence, I received one reply on April 4, 1899, and therefore, I am publishing some of the more interesting details.

Editor of "Svoboda"

* * * * * *

Papaikou, Hawaiian Islands
11 April, 1899

Reverend Father, Praised by Lord Jesus Christ!

We received your letter and two application forms for membership in the "Ukrainian" National Association," but one was lost and we do not know where it disappeared. Very often letters do not reach us and we have to send a letter of request, but as a rule we do not know to what post office to mail it. There are our people working for the post office and maybe they will mail postal inquiries to us.

Now I will inform you about our people. They are from the district of Chortkiw. In Papaikou there are 20 of us from the village of Kossiw (Kossow). In Onomea and Honomo there are eight young men from the village of Paushowka. There are also six from Slobidka. The rest of the people have been scattered among different islands, and we do not know the names of the plantations where they are. Later I shall write about them.

We were directed here by the agent Missler. He wrote letters to Western Ukraine (Halychyna) advising the people to come here — transportation was free; and the people listened to his advice and have now been dispersed among the different Hawaiian Islands.

The people here labor on the sugar cane plantations and earn $18.00 a month.

The work is so heavy that it is difficult to last a month; the cost of food is very high — what you earn, you leave in the store. It's the same servitude that once existed in Western Ukraine. Recently, on the 5th day of April, (1899), at six o'clock, five people tried to escape to San Francisco by a boat that was leaving for the Mainland. They were caught and had to pay a fine of $4.00 each. They asked their foreman if they could pay up their contract. He told them it would cost each man $100.00 — so they had to return to work and continue to slave.

Later we shall write more, and now we bow our heads in repsect, we Ukrainians from here and other places.

Mykola Holowaty[16]

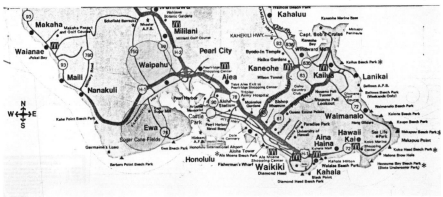

Map of southern part of Oahu showing Ewa and the location of Ewa and Waipalu plantations where the Ukrainian contract laborers worked in 1897-1900.

---

[16] L.S. Mykola Holowaty to Editory of "Svoboda" from Papaikou, H.I. 11 April, 1899. (translation)

Chapter 6

Investigation Dealing with Indentured Ukrainian Laborers

On the Island of Oahu, closer to the administrative centre of the Islands, the contract workers first complained of poor working conditions, then of maltreatment by the overseers; when no improvement seemd to be forthcoming they threatened to take strike action. This group for the most part, was composed of single men who were working in the sugar refineries. One day an unanticipated thing happened: a large number of lunas, assisted by the police and trustees from the local jail, descended on the refinery, and taking the protesting men by surprise, beat them with clubs and fists. As a consequence of this unprovoked attack on them, the men deserted. The planters, however, would not tolerate this situation and had the men arrested and brought before the magistrate; he imposed jail terms and heavy fines. In due time the ugly situation was reported to the press, and consequently, the Department of the Interior asked Dr. Chas. A. Peterson to investigate. He published his report on November 19, 1898.

After the first investigation, it would appear that it was difficult for Dr. Peterson to come to a conclusion and report in favor of the contract laborers who were imprisoned. Pressed, however, by the officials of the Territorial Government and the public opinion of those who were informed about the situation, he was forced to investigate further.

After making his second investigation, the Inspector of Immigration made a more detailed report to the president of the Board of Immigration.

Dr. Peterson's Report

Honolulu, July 5, 1899

Capt. J.A. King
President, Board of Immigration
Sir:

In view of the public interest just now developed in the case of the "Ukrainian" laborers who last November refused to work on the Oahu Plantation: and were by order of the Court imprisoned in Oahu Jail until such time as they would consent to return to work under their Contracts, in regard to which I had the honor to report to you at the time (See report of November 18, 1898) and at the request of Messrs, H. Hackfeld & Co., it has seemed best to supplement the report above mentioned, by further investigation.

Method of Investigation

In pursuance of this purpose, in my capacity as "Inspector of Immigrants" accompanied by interpreters and an impartial witness, I, on July 30th visited Oahu Plantation and interviewed twenty "Ukrainian" laborers still working on this estate. These men had been fellow passengers and collaborators with the prisoners now in Oahu Jail.

In order to forestall possible criticism, I will state that this investigation was held in the plantation office.

The only plantation employee present except the men interviewed was the plantation interpreter who came to this country with the men. I did not find it necessary to use him. One of the "Ukrainian" laborers who understood German was present throughout the inquiry and was directed to note any discrepancy between the German and "Ukrainian" interpreting.

Mr. N. Lakusta acted as "Ukrainian" interpreter and Mr. P. Keppler as German interpreter.

My questions were asked Mr. Keppler in English; Mr. Keppler in German asked the question of Mr. Lakusta and Mr. Lakusta interpreted into "Ukrainian" and the answer came back in reverse order.

Mr. Faneuf, Deputy Sheriff of Ewa and Wainanae, was present throughout the interview as a witness to the fact that no influence or intimidation on the part of anyone was evident.

I first took the names of those laborers who had complaints to make, and then questioned each one apart from his fellows.

The main questions asked were as follows:
1. Have you ever been ill treated on this plantation?
2. Have you ever seen any of your countrymen ill treated?
3. Are you satisfied that the terms of your contract have been fulfilled by the plantation?
4. If your contracts were cancelled today would you just as soon work here as elsewhere?
5. Do you, of your own knowledge, know of any cause of complaint, by reason of which your countrymen would prefer to remain in prison rather than return here?

Of the twenty men, four who said they had nothing to complain of, were not questioned further because of the lack of time.

As a result, of the sixteen questioned, I found *five* who complained of ill treatment and will consider them later.

Thirteen asserted that they had never seen any of their countrymen ill treated.

Thirteen considered that the terms of the contracts had been fulfilled by the plantation, two qualifying the answer, by saying they often were compelled to work overtime and while they were paid extra they did not think this was in their contract, and claimed that overtime worked disqualified them for work the next day.

Eleven would remain here if their contracts were cancelled.

Thirteen knew of no particular cause of complaint by reason of which those in Oahu Jail should refuse to work on Oahu Plantation.

> For convenience in designating the complainants I shall take the liberty of noting them by numbers.

> However, should it be necessary at any time to know the real name, I am sure the phonetic spelling in my notes will prove an accurate guide to identification.

The introduction to Dr. Peterson's report and his method of investigation are difficult to understand. From the start, it appears, that he was try to minimize the unsavory situation, and that there was an element of intimidation. He makes reference to impartial witnesses to forestall criticism, but there were none. However, as the inquiry was held in the Hackfeld Company office, in whose refinery the unmarried men were beaten, arrested and then imprisoned; and subsequently they received the "chain-gang" treatment by being marched to work every day under police supervision. The men testifying, therefore, it is reasonable to assume, would be rather timid to testify in detail. Another factor that may have caused them concern was the presence of the "interpreter", particularly if he were the someone who accompanied the laborers from Europe and informed the Hackfeld & Co., about the "ringleaders" who were trying to organize the men to attain the cancellation of their contracts. Fearing the consequences that may ensue, they testified with due care in order not to prejudice their situation more.

The fact that Dr. Peterson did not list the names of people interviewed, resorted to "phonetic spelling" and allotted numbers instead of names, would be viewed with suspicion — and his sincerey could also be questioned. It seems that he was attempting to forestall full disclosure.

Testimonies of Laborers

> No. 1 age 42. Married. Occupation in his own country was farming. Is quite well satisfied that the terms of his contract have been fulfilled by the plantation; except that he has to work rather hard, has to rise early, (5 a.m.) and is hurried by the overseer. Has a satifsactory house, plenty of wood, good water; can understand about half of what the overseer orders. When not understood the overseer by motions and examples explains. Does not take hold of the men. Formerly did, but not now.

> Has no complaint of ill treatment now. Some time ago an overseer who has now gone away and whose name is not known took witness by neck and pushed him away. Compelled to work overtime but is paid for it. Saw men ill treated at the time the single men went to Honolulu.

> The overseers struck the men with their fists; those men who were working about the boilers. (This refers to the episode mentioned in my former report where the man "Florentine" was knocked down.)

It appears clear that the report of Laborers No. 1, as made by Dr. Peterson for the remarks recorded are Dr. Peterson's own words. Nevertheless, the laborers objected to conditions of work: early rising and maybe working till sunset. There is no mention made that the plantation provided transportation to and from work. Overtime and Sunday work was expected.

Though the laborer seemed well-satisfied with living conditions, no mention is made that he was expected to buy his supplies in the plantation stores where prices were higher than in the stores in Honolulu.

As far as ill-treatment was concerned it is evident that the overseers used force and resorted to beating — grabbing men by the neck and pushing them. The men who were jailed were beaten with fists. Since there were 37 men jailed, the number of overseers must have been greater in number than the men to be able to overpower them. These were men in the employ of H. Hackfeld and Co. From the outset it appears that Dr. Peterson may have been on the side of the plantation owner; it is hard to understand why some of the overseers resorting to brutality were not brought in, cross examined by him under oath, and by the laborers and their responses reported. It is also difficult to understand why Hackfeld and Company would not provide the names of the overseers who were no longer available. Were they tranferred to another location to prevent questioning?

> No. 2 Age 48. Married. Farmer. A crippled rheumatic who has worked now and then for the last four months. His complaint is: that a fellow workman has turned informer and told the overseer that he, No. 2, had complained because he was compelled to work Sunday, whereupon the overseer came to him while he was alone and knocked his head against the boiler and holding a hammer to his head had threatened to kill him. This was five months ago. The overseer had left the plantation, and he could not identify him. Has been treated well ever since.

There is no doubt that conditions on the plantation and in the small "community" were not happy, and there may have been cases of ill-feelings among the workers. In the case of Laborer No. 2, it is evident that work in the irrigated fields and around the boilers in hot rooms increased the intensity of his rheumatic condition.

Being compelled to work on Sunday placed the laborers in the category of slaves — in their native land, even during the period of serfdom, the peasant-farmers were able to be free from work and attend church. Although there was no church for them in Hawaii, the laborers needed Sunday as a day of rest, but this, it seems, was denied them. In the case of Laborer No. 2, the overseer was not available, and for the convenience, no doubt, disappeared. Since Laborer No. 2 only worked "now and then" and as he was only paid for days he worked; he, no doubt, barely earned enough to buy food for his family and if he did not earn enough, got into debt!

> No. 3, Age 24. Single. Farmer. About three months after arriving here, in December last, while at work was slapped in the face by the overseer for nothing. Left the field and on his way home was met by the head overseer who jumped from his horse and kicked him until he fell down. He was helped to his home and arrested for assault upon the overseer; taken to Court and fined $18.00 and sent to prison for 36 days. There were only Japanese witnesses. They would not testify for him, but were against him. Since that time has been treated well.

Has never seen any of his countrymen ill treated. If his contract was cancelled, would leave at once. Has been fined in Court three times.

Laborer No. 3 was not only assaulted by overseers on two occasions — and on the same day, but was also fined and sent to jail for 36 days. Actually he was fined three times. If one fine was eighteen dollars, three fines, no doubt, absorbed all his earnings. It was regrettable that the Japanese laborers who saw the assault would not testify on his behalf — there is no doubt that they feared the "lash": the cowwhip, evidently was used without hesitation; but in the case of Laborer No. 3, it was the rope. Kicking a worker when he was down was a lowdown cowardly act. Why the head overseer was not summoned to testify is incomprehensible; this shows that the conduct of the Inspector of Immigrants was far from unbiased. He also failed to record his disapproval of such action, and failed to summon Herr Hackfeld to ascertain if he was aware of the unmanly behavior of his overseers and whether he gave them orders to carry out acts of brutality. It appears that Hackfeld and Company should have been charged. There is a possibility that Laborer No. 3 may have taken "disciplinary" action against the overseer, in retaliation for being slapped, and this resulted in the action taken by the "head overseer". It is true that workers could not testify that they saw others maltreated — the men were, no doubt, singled out in the tall sugar cane, or other places, and beaten as Laborer No. 3 was.

No. 4 Age 51. Married. Farm Laborer, says: He has been whipped by an overseer who was discharged last week.

He was unloading cane when the overseer struck him with a stick of cane on the side of the head bruising and breaking the skin, for no reason.

Says: This was witnessed by a fellow countryman "Hekatchu Proko." Made no complaint.

Says: All overseers whip the men. Cannot specify any man or any overseer, but there is no overseer here now who has whipped the men.

Has been fined once in Court; the above Hekatchu Proko was called and testified that he had never seen any of his countrymen ill treated. That he did not see anyone strike No. 4 with a cane. Was told so by No. 4.

Worker No. 4 would not be intimidated and testified that all three men were whipped. The fact they he could not give the name of the overseer is understandable, as he did not know English language well enough. All Dr. Peterson had to do was to request the office to provide the name of the discharged overseer. If No. 4 was fined in the Court, the Court records were available. It is understandable, too, why he could not name the other workers if they happened to be Chinese or Japanese. Hekatchu Proko*, it seems, turned "yellow" and was afraid to testify. Dr. Peterson's spelling of names and his "phonetics", too, appear to be faulty. Hekatchu Proko was

* Lakawczuk, Prokop was from the village of Navorzhanka.

very likely "Lakawczuk Prokop", as Lukawczuk was the only Prokop among the indentured workers from the Ukraine on the passenger list.

> No. 5 Says: After being here two weeks (This was in September, 1898) was digging a trench and had removed his boots. While putting his boots on again, an overseer came along and struck him on the head with a rope and then jumping from his horse knocked No. 5 into the ditch. Only Japanese witnesses, and could not identify them or the offending overseer. He complained to the interpreter. He has seen those of his countrymen who are now in prison, ill treated, but cannot specify any of them.

> Says: Pachko, Olexa was whipped by overseer who whipped those in jail.

The Japanese laborers were not interested in testifying, and their behaviour may be interpreted as unmanly; but, it is understood, that the Japanese laborers wanted to see the European and other laborers get into trouble and leave, so that eventually the whole field of sugar cane labour supply could be filled by the Japanese, and then they would be able to command better bargaining opportunities.

Since No. 5 complained to the interpreter — and he was present during the investigation — he should have been asked to testify under oath. "Pachko Olexa"* it would appear, either wanted to engratiate himself or was afraid to give testimony against the overseer. He, it would seem, was anxious to work out the term of his contract so he would be able to leave unimpeded for the Mainland. He simply stated, as reported by Dr. Peterson, that:

> ...he has no complaints to make. Was once shaken by an overseer when he was stupid, but nothing to speak of.

Though Oleska Pachkow appears to represent the servile type of laborer — the planters wanted — who was conditioned on the "lords estate", in his native village of Kotsubynchyky to do "fieldwerk" without protest, his attitude, however, in Hawaii in not wanting to give evidence against the plantation officials may be better understood if one takes into consideration that he, age 33, and his wife Olena, age 27, had three children to support, ages 8, 4, and 2, and if Mr. Pachkow would get imprisoned, like the others, his family would be left destitute — as with a two year old child Mrs. Pachkow would not have been able to go to work. Dr. Peterson's biased and inadequate summation of the testimonies was as follows:

> I have given the text of the complaints in full because they are typical of those made in the Police Court in Honolulu in November, 1898, at the trial of the "Ukrainians" now in question. (prison?)

> I have no doubt the story of No. 1 is true; that he was taken by the neck and pushed, but probably not without some cause; and we are left with the uncertainty as to time, as to offender and without witnesses.

---

* The passenger list has the name of an Oleksa Pachkow (Pachkiw) — Dr. Peterson's phonetics required improvement.

The complaint of No. 2 is just as impossible of proof as that of No. 1. The case of No. 3 had had the benefit of Court proceedings, and with an offender charged and witnesses against, with no defence, we could expect nothing other than the outcome he states. Whatever the original trouble I am inclined to believe he was slapped and kicked.

The story of attack on the way home and arrest for assault after trouble in the fields bears the impress of a time honored method on some plantations. But this belief cannot right the matter.

No. 4 was unfortunate in his witnesses and his general statement scarcely merited credence.

No. 5 only showed, while there might be basis for his complaint, a tendency to exaggerate.

The results of this investigation seems, therefore, meagre and to change in no way the status of the "Ukrainians" now in prison, as presented in my report of November 1. We find there are some "Ukrainians" content to labor on this plantation, who acknowledge good treatment and express no sympathy for those in prison. These are nearly all married men.

We find that since the strike of last November, whatever the policy previously, there has been evidence of special care not to touch the men,, at least openly, and in general a policy of giving no cause for complaint. At the same time, to be fair to complaining ones, one cannot be but impressed with the possibility of shrewd calculations in the selection of time, place and occasion in which ill treatment might be practised with impunity. While not bearing directly upon this case it may be a matter of interest to note that the three men: Manjetski, Piste Pendras and Teper Jacob, named in my report of November as leaders, are now free and have been made prominent through newspaper mention.

Manjetski lately attempted to shoot himself and his wife because of his co-conspirator Pendras had abused his confidence. The newspapers gave a detailed account of this affair.

Teper Jacob is the man who gained the sympathy of Rabbi Levy and was freed through Mr. Levy's endeavors. Those remaining in prison are upheld by the idea that they have a case for damages against either the plantation or the government for imprisonment.

Respectfully Submitted.

(Signed) Chas. A. Peterson, M.D.

Inspector of Immigrants

Before Dr. Peterson concluded his report, some Ukrainian laborers managed to have enough money to buy their freedom and they immediately left for the Mainland where they established contact with their countrymen in San Francisco, one of them being Rev. Abapius Honcharenko. He gained the co-operation of freedom loving citizens, and editors of the San Fran-

---

[1] Hawaii State Archives, Honolulu, H. I.

cisco press, and exposed the exploitation tactics of the Hawaiian planters. The press, needing more information on the situation, initiated its own investigation and sent Rabbi Levy to Hawaii.

Just as Dr. Peterson published his report, copies of the "San Francisco Examiner" arrived in Hawaii and he felt it incumbent on himself to add more facts which are embodied in his letter of August 2, 1899:

Honolulu, August 2nd, 1899

Capt. J.A. King
President, Board of Immigration

Sir:

Since closing my report of July 31st, with the reference to the "Ukrainians" on Oahu Plantation, there has come to my notice a lurid article in the San Francisco Examiner of July 24th entitled "Slavery in Hawaii under the American Flag." Therefore, I am led to add a few facts. Many of those who testified on the 30th ult. claimed to have saved money during their service. Postal Bank books were shown containing $30.00, $40.00 and $50.00. A twenty dollar saving was said to be hidden away in a stocking — $65.00 had been paid on a $85.00 advance.

The passage was free according to contract and had only to be paid in case the contract was cancelled.

Jacob Teper referred to this article by Rabbi Levy, as an intelligent man conversant with the German and "Ukrainian" languages, signed a contract printed in both these languages, to work as an agricultural laborer, and now claims he understood he has to work as a cabinet maker. This is the man named in my previous reports and under oath in the Police Court testified that he had not complained to Mr. Hackfeld, the Austrian Consul; and his complaint was that he had been called by a number instead of his name, dogs in his country being so designated.

That he had no other complaint against the plantation and that if his contract was cancelled he would be perfectly willing to go back to Oahu Plantation to work. But not otherwise.

Respectfully Submitted,
(Signed) Chas. A. Peterson, M.D. [2]
Inspector of Immigrants

Peterson's Addenda

During his investigation Dr. Peterson was able to discover that some of the laborers had money in their possessions — Postal Bank books showed that they contained $30.00, $40.00 and $50.00. Some of his officials, it seems,

---

[2] Ibid.

had gone as far as to search the people to determine the money they carried on their person and found $20.00 hidden in a stocking. He did not want to say whether the person or persons found with the money was a man or a woman, but since the money was found in a stocking, it was likely that women were subjected to such a personal search.

The Inspector of Immigration, Dr. Peterson, made reference to the fact that passage was free to the Island, but does not elucidate on the fact, that is, that the money the peasants had to pay for their passage from Bremen to Canada should have been available, but since some only had $30 - $50 in their Postal Bank books, it may well be concluded that they spent all they earned for food and clothing — in the company stores — and used most of their money they had available for paying for their passage to Canada amounting to about $110.00 per person and half fare for each child.* That was not a very satifactory way of getting established in a New Country.

It does not appear fair for the investigator to single out the Jewish laborer, Jacob Teper who testified under oath that he had not complained to Mr. Hackfeld, the Austrian Consul. If Jacob Teper perjured himself in court, it would suggest that fearing the consequences — and he did: He was imprisoned with the Ukrainian laborers, the single men with whom he came to Hawaii.

Whether the Inspector of Immigration would refer to any article in the ''San Francisco Examiner'' as lurid, is difficult to understand. This, however, will be made possible for the reader to determine for himself when he read the material, ''Slavery in Hawaii''.

Chinese contract workers cutting sugar cane.

---

* Married couples that planned to go to Canada must have, on the average, brought from $400. to $500. with them to Hawaii.

Chapter 7

"The Examiner" of San Francisco to the Rescue

Immediately after Dr. Peterson completed his investigation and reported his findings on July 31, 1899, it appears that the newspapers from the Mainland reached Honolulu, among them "The Examiner"[1], carried a two-issue report on the contract laborers, based on Rabbi M.S. Levy's investigation. Consequently, Dr. Peterson felt impelled to amend his report with further inocuous observations. The report, which appeared in "The Examiner" substantiated the complaints made by the laborers and the information provided to the authorities and politicians by Rev. I.I. Ardan, editor of the Ukrainian "Svoboda" (Liberty).

It appears, therefore, that three clergymen: Rev. Nestor Dmytriw, editor, Rev. I.I. Ardan, Rev. Ahapius Honcharenko; and a San Francisco Rabbi: M.S. Levy, through their genuine efforts eventually succeeded in getting the "Ukrainian" contract workers and others released from Hawaiian bondage.

The first two were Ukrainian Catholic clergymen, Rev. Honcharenko was a Ukrainian Orthodox refugee clergyman and Rabbi Levy, a well-known Jewish pulpit orator in San Francisco, who, it appears, may have come from Western Ukraine and knew the Ukrainian language. There is no doubt, too, that in San Francisco, Rev. Honcharenko and Rabbi Levy were acquaintances. Ahapius Honcharenko had close connections with the editors of some San Francisco papers, and knew the plight of "coolie" contract workers in Hawaii; and having objected to print to the treatment of the Chinese labor,* was the right person to induce an investigation of conditions of "Ukrainian" contract laborers in Hawaii. As a result, therefore, on his requests "The Examiner" sent Rabbi Levy to Hawaii to make an on the spot investigation. Subsequently, "The Examiner" published two lengthy articles, the first bearing the following headlines:

SLAVERY IN HAWAII
UNDER THE AMERICAN FLAG

Thirty-Six Serfs, Who Fled From Plantations, Imprisoned Beneath Oahu's Bloodhound Banner.

* See "Alaska Scrapbook," microfilm, University of California, Oakland
[1] The Examiner of San Francisco, July 24, 1899.

The Prison on the Reef at Honolulu

> Where runaway slaves from the plantations are confined until they agree to return to the cane and coffee fields or pay in money the price of their freedom to their masters. Over the entrance to the prison is the significant figure of a bloodhound trailing a fugitive.[2]

Slavery and involuntary servitude of the most degrading type exist in the Hawaiian Islands today as a means for enforcement of contracts made by laborers to work on sugar and coffee plantations. Thirty-six "Ukrainians", subjects of the Austrian empire, are now confined to Oahu prison, Honolulu because they refused to comply longer with the onerous conditions imposed on them by their owners. They were convicted of "deserting contract service" and were sentenced to indefinite imprisonment. They can gain release only by buying their way out of jail or going back to the cane-fields. Their tale is told by Rabbi M.S. Levy of this city. It is one to cause anger and astonishment among those that boast that freedom lives wherever floats the American flag.[3]

"The Examiner" also quoted Amendment XIII United States Constitution which reads:

> Neither slavery nor involuntary servitude, except as a punishment for crime whereof the party shall have been duly convicted, shall exists within the United States or any place subject to their jurisdiction.[4]

And who were these thirty-seven slaves referred to by "The Examiner"? They were the Ukrainian immigrants (a group of "Sifton Settlers") on their way to gain freedom and land ownership on the Canadian prairies; who claimed they were deceived and diverted from going to Canada to become contract workers in Hawaii, and refusing to accept unfair conditions of employment were imprisoned. "Miserable slaves," says 'The Examiner,' who, "as a consequence of having the manly fortitude to resist oppression, are held in servitude even more degrading than that which existed in the Southern States four decades ago."[5]

The article refers to them as "bondsmen of the soil," and "peons of the plantations," who were not "ignorant savages from the depths of Africa, nor semi-civilized natives of the Gold Coast, but white men and white women. . .victims of as hard a set of slave driving bullies as ever disgraced the name of man."[6]

Credit is due to an American newspaper in San Francisco, enjoying the "freedom of the press," dared to condemn the agents of the "Big Five" sugar cane operators in Hawaii in such strong language. The denunciation of the planters and their associates — "the profiteers and exploiters" — makes interesting reading.

---

[2] Ibid.

[3] Ibid.

[4] "The Examiner", July 24, 1899.

[5] Ibid.

[6] Ibid.

"The Examiner's" Appraisal of Hawaiian Contract Laborers

The story of the contract laborers of Hawaii is one of deception, cruelty, and oppression. It is a tale of men and women who, induced by promises of a livelihood in the beautiful islands of the South Pacific, and assured of safety and justice from the fact that the American flag will wave above them, are entrapped into conditions which they cannot overcome, and the infraction of which is followed by penal servitude.

The contract laborers of the Hawaiian Islands are slaves and serfs in fact in name. Police run them down should they attempt to escape and district magistrates promptly convict them for "deserting contract service."

Thirty-six "Ukrainian" contract laborers — are now within the walls. It is nothing that their imprisonment is in direct conflict with the Constitution and the laws of the United States. The flag floats above Honolulu, but the banner of the trailing bloodhound, and now the Stars and Stripes, indicates the law of the land.[7]

Jacob Teper

However there were 37 laborers imprisoned at the "Reef," the additional one was Jacob Teper who was not of Ukrainian extraction, but a Jew who came to Hawaii with one of the Hawaiian groups.

It appears in order to observe that the Jewish immigrants that left Europe and travelled to the New World — since they were fewer in number — often travelled with the Ukrainians. They knew the Ukrainian language and were accepted and well treated by the larger group.

Therefore, on visiting the Ukrainians in the Oahu Jail, Rabbi Levy established contact with him. Jacob Teper not only provided information but produced certain documents; the most important one being the contract which had been preserved. All the contract laborers were obliged to carry the contract on their person and any fines imposed on the laborers were recorded on those documents.[8]

Jacob Teper's contract, like those of the other 36 laborers, was made between him and Oahu Sugar Co., of which the Austrian Consul in Hawaii, Hackfeld was a director — and in this case, the *Master*; and Jacob Teper, the servant. The master-servant relationship was outlined in detail and published in full by "The Examiner."

When Rabbi Levy visited the "Reef" he was approached by the "serf,"
· Jacob Teper. The Rabbi had an opportunity to talk to the Ukrainian laborers, that were incarcerated in the "Honolulu Alcatraz"; and also secured copies of the documents carried by the laborer, Jacob Teper. "The Examiner" had the last page carrying the record of Teper's fine published. (The Teper contract was identical to that of the contract of Andruch Werbicki who arrived in Hawaii with the first contingent.)

Rabbi Levy was impressed with Jacob Teper's story and went to the Austrian and German Consul in Hawaii, Mr. Hackfeld, to ascertain the

[7] Ibid.
[8] Ibid.

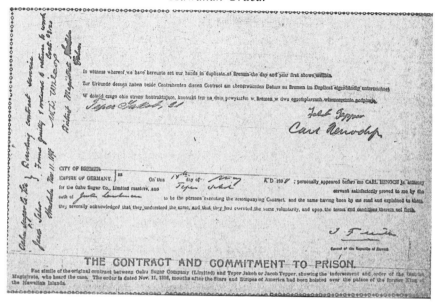

THE CONTRACT AND COMMITMENT TO PRISON.

Fac simile of the original contract between Oahu Sugar Company (Limited) and Teper Jakob or Jacob Tepper, showing the indorsement and order of the District Magistrate, who heard the case. The order is dated Nov. 11, 1898, months after the Stars and Stripes of America had been hoisted over the palace of the former King of the Hawaiian Islands.

Jacob Teper: Deserting contract service. Found guilty and ordered to return to work. Cost $8.00. Nov. 11, 1898. W. L. Wilcox, District Magistrate, Honolulu Oahu.

amount of money that was required to secure his countryman's release from slavery. When informed that the amount was $120.00, Rabbi Levy took the next step:

> I went to work among some of my friends in Honolulu and got them interested in the case. We succeeded in raising the money. I took the money to Hackfeld and paid him, as you may see by his receipt. Apparently, he acted as the agent of the Oahu Company, in receipting for the money. You may easily imagine the sort of sympathy or assistance that an Austrian or a German subject would get in a dispute with the company from an official maintaining such relations.[9]

Rabbi Levy also expressed sincere sympathy for the Ukrainian laborers who, he stated, would have to remain in prison unless people of good will and means could be found to raise 36 times $120.00 to buy their freedom, or that the American Constitution would come into force in Hawaii and declare them free.

Once Jacob Teper became free, he secured employment in Honolulu at a wage of $3.00 a day.

"The Examiner" also published the receipt for Teper's release, signed by Mr. Hackfeld.

---

[9] Ibid.

American People Startled

When "The Examiner" exposed the horrendous treatment of the Ukrainian contract laborers in Hawaii, the American people were startled and so were the Hawaiians who worked hard to achieve the annexation of the Islands — adding them to the "Land of the Free". However, as "The Examiner" stated, the treatment meted out to the laborers was slavery and "insults our flag."[11] The second article of exposure was three columns in width, which included a photograph showing the Ukrainian laborers dressed in prison garb working under the surveillance of a prison guard with a gun in hand.

The situation in the "reef penitentiary" was a definite insult to the Stars and Stripes which replaced the flags of the Hawaiian Territories, which in turn replaced the standard, bearing the Union Jack of the British, which was used by Kamehameha and his descendants (who once accepted temporarily the standard "flag" of the Russian czar). Slavoery existed under the former flag, but the freedom loving Americans, no doubt, did not anticipate that it would continue under the administration of the planters and the "Big Five".

PRICE PAID FOR A
WHITE SLAVE'S FREEDOM

MONEY THAT BOUGHT A WHITE MAN'S LIBERTY.

The original of the receipt given to Rabbi Levy by the agents of the plantation where Jacob Teper was a contract laborer.

Honolulu, H.I., July 3rd, 1899. Received of Rev. Levy the sum of One hundred twenty dollars, for release of Yacob Teper (contract laborer) in Oahu Sugar Co.

---

[10] Ibid.

[11] "The Examiner", July 25, 1899.

Contract Laborers working as convicts on Oahu Island.

Contract Labor Practices a Blot on Civilization

The first paragraph of the second report is a strong condemnation of the "contract labor" practices in Hawaii, labelling them as a "blot on civilization."

The reaction that came from the politicians shows that — American flag or no flag — barbaric laws permitting slavery in Hawaii were still in force; and before the laborer could attain freedom, Congress had to act. This was clearly stated by Congressman Eugene F. Loud:

Must Look to Congress

The laws of Hawaii are still in force. Hawaii was annexed by treaty. One provision stipulated that the laws of Hawaii should govern that country until the American Congress adopted a code of laws to displace them. Things there are still in a chaotic condition, and will be for some time to come. Hawaii is a part of the United States — and is not. That sounds paradoxical, but the fact remains.

During the last session of Congress the Administration urged the adoption of measures that would relieve just such conditions as were brought to light in the publication made possible by Rabbi Levy's investigations. But Congress had such a mass of business to transact, it was impossible to take up provisions relative to conditions in Hawaii. Under the circumstances, all that could possibly be done has been done. No further steps can be taken until suitable laws have been passed. I am assured that the next Congress will afford relief for all existing hardships by proper enactment.

Eugene F. Loud
Congressman Fifth Congressional District[12]

Surely no American dreamed that when the Stars and Stripes replaced the Hawaiian flag last year that there was actual slavery on the Islands. Many knew that there was a contract labor law and that the plantations were worked by contract laborers; but no one ever whispered before that the penitentiary on Oahu Island — the reef prison — was used to imprison the laborers indefinitely when they failed to live up to their iron-bound contracts. Still the truth has come out at last and the first details of the barbarism, the fiendish inhumanity, have been revealed through "The Examiner" on the information of a San Francisco rabbi, the Rev. M.S. Levy. Well may the people exclaim against such traffic in human bodies and demand that the infamy be terminated at the earliest moment. Nothing worse, nothing so bad was ever enacted in the slavery days of the South as to throw the poor serf into jail with criminals untried, unheard, without prospect of release and with the knowledge that the longer he remains in prison the more oppressive becomes the debt for which he is imprisoned.

The publication of the facts, the form of contract, the receipt for the price of freedom for a poor Galician Hebrew named Jacob Teper, carried conviction with them. There was no doubting the story, no palliation that could be offered for such a thing under any flag the world over and least of all under the foremost emblem of liberty, the Stars and Stripes.[13]

Congressman Julius Kahn also expressed his opposition to the conditions of slavery to which the Ukrainian and other contract laborers were subjected. Among the Europeans there was also the Portuguese, Spanish, and Polish workers, and among those from Asia and the Islands the Chinese, Japanese, Korean and Filipinos. The congressman stated:

Slaves Must Be Set Free

If these men have gone to the Islands under erroneous impressions of existing circumstances; and if, on their arrival, they found that they were being treated as slaves, they had the right to run away. And if there is no present way of securing their release from prison, this Government must make a way — and must make it soon.

It seems to me that efforts should be made at once to secure the release of these persons under habeas corpus proceedings. I doubt but that the men could be

---

[12] Ibid.
[13] Ibid.

set at liberty under such proceedings. I am satisfied Congress will take up these questions at an early day, and I have an abiding faith that American statesmanship will be able to secure justice for all of the people of the Islands.

The efforts made by the agents of these plantations to secure laborers by contract in Europe would be put down at once. No doubt in the case of Yacob Teper glittering inducements were held out to him to enter into such a contract. The wage offered, expressed in the money of his own country, is equivalent to seventy-five marks, which is a very respectable salary. These agents are the real culprits, and should be severely dealt with.

Julius Kahn
Congressman Fourth Congressional District[14]

In concluding the article of July 25, the editor of "The Examiner" used very strong language to impress on the reader the dastardly acts of the planters and the administration.

Men are imprisoned untried and indefinitely and the longer they stay in prison the greater becomes the penalty. A common thief serves his time, pays his debt to the State, and steps out of the penitentiary a free man-nay, more if he behave himself he will get credits and when his shortened time is up he gets clothes and money. These contract laborers are in a far worse plight. Imprisonment under such conditions is horrible. The crime is not commensurate with the punishment and no American, no Anglo-Saxon could ever tolerate such a thing no matter how prone the offender was to desert his contract.

Can one imagine anything more contemptible than to bring over these poor peasants on such contracts as these and then having got them here to make them abject slaves? True they may get bigger pay than they could earn at home; but at least no man threw them into prison there without some sort of trial. Not one of those poor fellows had been in prison less than eight months and not one can get out until his debt is paid. The agents in Europe are the culprits who should be punished for sending the poor peasants out to the islands.[15]

---

[14] "The Examiner", July 25, 1899
[15] Ibid.

Chapter 8

State of Servitude Continues

Though the articles about "Slavery in Hawaii" published in the July 1899 issue of "The Examiner" of San Francisco, and in other American papers, created considerable uneasiness in some American political circles, and considerable consternation among the American liberals, little was done to help the Hawaiian contract workers.

It is very likely that the religious groups and welfare organizations may also have been perplexed, to learn that the new State of Hawaii, only recently admitted into the Union with the leading democracy of the World, would disregard any suggestion that its planters stooped to socially repugnant acts and retrogressive behavior by exploiting labor and maintaining the contract laborers under a state of indenture. It was the bondage of the European people who were brought into the country through deception of corrupt agents. Yet until 1900, the governmental authorities in Hawaii, seemed to pay little heed to the situation and took no action to rectify conditions.

Inspector General of Schools in Hawaii Concerned

When "The Examiner" prepared for publication its report based on Rabbi Levy's investigation of the contract labor situation in Hawaii, it was also able to interview Henry S. Townsend, Inspector-General of Schools in Hawaii, who at that time was attending the National Education Convention in Los Angeles. He evinced strong concern over the exploitation of the contract workers stating:

> I have intended all along to lay before "The Examiner" just such facts as the investigations of the Rabbi Levy have revealed; but have been too busy. Now, if this matter is brought before Congress there will be an end to that which many of us have fought vainly for years. No very serious attempts have been made to kill this law in the Hawaiian Legislature because the interests of the planters were always too heavy and persuasive. In the courts the best endeavors have been put forth and one case questioning the constitutionality of the law was carried to the Supreme Court. Sanford B. Dole, who was then one of the judges, wrote a strong opinion against the law; but his two asssociates were in favor of it. Within the past two months a case has been decided in the Islands and in sustaining the law again it was held the United States Constitution is not yet in force in all its provisions.[1]

Townsend continued to stress the fact that the contract labor system in operation also tended to bring in more and more Japanese to the Islands, and concluded that the repressive labor contract should be abolished.

---

[1] "The Examiner" July 25, 1899.

A curious result of McKinley's desire to settle the squabble between Japan and Hawaii is now noticeable. The Japanese Government was paid $75,000.00 damages for the attempted exclusion of the "Japs" and it was hoped that this would deter them from coming to Hawaii. They used to arrive at the rate of a hundred a month, now they are coming at the rate of 1,000 a month and there will be trouble some day to control this immigration. However, one thing at a time, "The Examiner" will accomplish great things if it induces Congress to knock out the contract labor law as soon as it meets, and so end a blot on the civilizaton there.[2]

"The Examiner" shows that a small group of Ukrainian contract laborers in resisting "Hawaiian bondage" were able to induce the President of the Mighty Republic to take firm action to eradicate vestiges of slavery in Hawaii. "The Examiner" also criticizes the attitude of the former Consul-General Wilder by stating that his views on existing slavery in the Islands were different from those of a disinterested educated man:

> How different is the view of a gentleman who has always been close to the planters and was the last to represent the Hawaiian Government officially in this city. He explains and apologizes; but denies nothing of the facts and so former Consul-General Wilder of Hawaii is inclined to believe that Rabbi M.S. Levy has allowed his sympathies to get away with his judgement. He said yesterday:[3]

The former Consul-General also resorted to the racist and other derogatory remarks about immigrants — remarks used often in the U.S.A., and later adopted in Canada.

> These are the dirtiest and among the laziest people on the face of the globe.* I don't wonder that thirty-six of them are in the prison on the reef and I don't believe they would be grateful to be released. They have a better time in the prison than out of it. The food is good and the work light and after 4 p.m. the prisoners can loll about a fine shady court and take their ease in place of working ten or more hours a day in the plantations and sugar factories ... they have all they want to eat and little to do, and that just suits the "Ukrainians".[4]

It is difficult to understand how such assertions could be made as the men, in prison, though dressed in prison garb could utilize the available prison facilities for keeping clean. They were in no way any more unclean than the other prisoners, and as far as being lazy, that had never been the trait of the "Ukrainian" and other European immigrants. However, when someone studies the pictures of the imprisoned contract workers with the overseer, gun in hand, supervising their activities, and in like manner formerly the plantation overseer with cow-whip in hand was setting the pace, one can't

---

[2] Ibid.

[3] Ibid.

[4] Ibid.

* Frank Oliver, the Canadian Member of Parliament, spoke in the same derogatory manner about the European immigrants, and his statements in the Aug. 15, 1899 issue of the Daily Miner, Nelson, B.C. were reprinted in a Hawaiian paper.

help but come to the conclusion that Consul-General Wilder's observations were not in accordance with facts. And besides the prison officials made these observations about the imprisoned Ukrainian laborers that contradict his virulent assertions:

> They are not bad or rebellious men who object to work of any sort...they make model prisoners. But they will not work under conditions provided by the Oahu Sugar Company.[5]

Rabbi Levy reported further:

> When I was at Honolulu, I had occasion to visit the reef. That is the Island prison of Oahu, where all classes of offenders, murderers, felons, and misdemeanants are confined at hard labor. While I was there my attention was drawn to thirty-seven who were confined because they had refused to fulfill their contracts to labor for the Oahu plantation. They were dressed in stripes like the other prisoners. They were made to do the same labor in the quarries and on the roads. They were conveyed about the Islands in a public vehicle, accompanied by armed guards. In fact, they were made to suffer all the indignities and pains of a felon under sentence.[6]

During the last days of the nineteenth century, the Oahu prison, generally called the "Reef", was an island penitentiary where, it appears, the inmates had no rights and few privileges; where freedom accorded prisoners in more advanced countries of the Western World were nonexistent. That was the prison where the striking "Ukrainian" laborers were incarcerated. And they emigrated to attain more freedom!!

Oahu Prison, "The Reef" Honolulu (Bishop Museum)

---

[5] "The Examiner" Ibid.
[6] Ibid.

Hope for Freedom Gleaming on the Horizon

That on the majority of plantations the contract workers were exploited to a degree, may be deduced from a statement made by one of the managers, who admitted that the fining of laborers failing to meet the foreman's conception of proper work led to considerable injustice.[7] Since the wages were low, and the fines heavy, the laborer often was unable to meet his indebtedness in the plantation store — and the more he objected, the more the fines increased — and therefore, even if his term of contract expired, the laborer was unable to become free until he paid-up his debt. There isn't much evidence that many laborers were financially able to buy their freedom in the same manner Yacob Teper did and, therefore, many had extreme difficulty in extricating themselves from their Hawaiian bondage. It was Teper's own people who paid for his release from contract, but there was no religious group or social agency that was prepared to secure the release of those Ukrainians unable to pay for their clearance from contract. Some had to remain longer on the plantations. One person, however, did not abandon efforts to help his countrymen. He was Rev. I.I. Ardan, the editor of "Svoboda." Though his organization, the present Ukrainian National Association, was not able to assist the people financially — it could now — Ardan continued to inform the Ukrainian-Hawaiian laborers and encouraged them with the articles in "Svoboda" — likely the only paper the Ukrainians in Hawaii read.

The Ukrainian people who chose to emigrate in order to avoid being subjected to further oppression by the Hapsburgs and the Romanovs, refused to accept the laws of Kamehameha which kept them in servitude; and Rev. Ardan, a true liberal, continued to write about their plight. Since no accurate statistical data was available about the numbers of his people who came to Hawaii, he repeated the same number time and again, and at times, kept repeating information he had used before:

> There are about 350 of our people in the Hawaiian Islands at present (among them are several Poles). They are scattered in small groups among the Hawaiian Islands in order to prevent them from being able to plan strike actions — which, to tell the truth, will not help them very much.[8]

Ardan also restated unfair conditions of work:

> They work a 14-hour day in the country where it is very hot. Each day they are made to carry ploughs to the fields weighing about 160 pounds for a distance of nearly three miles and in addition they have to bear constantly the derision and torment from their overseers.[9]

It is difficult to understand why the men were forced to carry ploughs to the fields, unless this was a type of "pack drill" to provoke the men to react

---

[7] Curtis, Adler
[8] "Svoboda", February 15, 1900.
[9] Ibid.

by refusing to do so, and hence that there could be a reason to impose heavy fines. Another observation made by Rev. Ardan about laborers taking their wives to fields to work beside them is not clear. Whether this was done to have the women earn a little money so that the family would be able to clear its indebtedness sooner, or that this was done for the safety of the women.

The Ukrainians and Poles, in many cases, were unfortunate to work for the Austrian planters who still considered their laborers to be Austrian subjects, and therefore, obliged to carry out all orders of the "Hackfelds".

Another problem which created gross unfairness was fines imposed when laborers became ill. The "Svoboda" reported: "If a person gets ill, they do not believe him and impose a $5-$10 fine, or a 20-day prison term." Under such conditions the fines deprived the family of the much needed financial support. Men were, therefore, justified in taking strike action and like the Chinese and others, the Ukrainian laborers attempted other means of escaping from the excessively harsh conditions of work. Ardan added:

> At the present time four men are in jail for desertion and, for trying to get work in another plantation. However, Hawaii consists of islands, each being surrounded by water so one is not able to escape far. Our escaping countrymen were, therefore, caught before long, and when apprehended by the mounted policemen, were kicked like dogs, beaten over the head, neck and shoulders with ropes and then were tied to the horses and forced to walk behind the mounted policeman.

Hope For Freedom

> Hope for freedom, however, for our Hawaiian-Ukrainians, is beginning to gleam brighter on the horizon. The Austrian Consular office in Philadelphia informed me that progress has been made in the matter of our slaves; and R.R. Hitt, chairman of the committee for External Affairs, and the author of a Bill for the admittance of the Hawaiian Territories into the Union writes that if his Bill is approved, the laborers in Hawaii will be as free as the laborers in Pennsylvania or any other state in the United States. It is true that there is a Bill introduced by R.R. Hitt, and as well in another Bill introduced by the Senate to deal with this same matter: (the freeing of laborers from their contracts); but at the same time there is a paragraph in this Bill which states that all contracts made before the passage of the Bill will continue to be in force. This seems to mean that the laborers who signed their contracts prior to the passage of the new law, must remain in the state of slavery until they have worked off the indebtedness to the planters (likely the cost of transportation provided) but Mr. R.R. Hitt says nothing about this, and maybe that the contract workers will be an exception this time. *If this were to be so, then the Hawaiian-Ukrainians would become more or less free in the month of July,* * *for; Senator Culton has moved that this Bill become law the 4th of July of this year, (1900).*

> Recently, I was able to contact several prominent Senators and Representatives in this matter and as soon as I receive their replies, I shall hasten to inform our Hawaiians through the medium of "Svoboda".

---

* They, of course, had to meet their store accounts.

I also presented, in writing, the whole matter to the League of Social Service attaching the necessary information, and as far as I was able, based it on available factual material. The league is composed of very influential and active people from among the Protestants who have as their objective the policy of helping those in social misery.

In brief, there is hope for the freeing of our Hawaiians. However, in the mean time one should remember that the planters are not sleeping but are exerting all possible means, as we learn Mr. Sewell who is a special agent of the United States in Hawaii, to present the situation of contract workers in the Islands mentioned in the best light, and are also trying to prove that the laborers are well-cared-for and satisfied, and that it would be better to leave the whole matter as it was previously.

What are the Hawaiian-Ukrainians to do?

In view of the attitude taken by the planters, the Hawaiian-Ukrainians neither have to "rejoice" too soon, nor to remain silent or just take steps to provide us with brief general information about their situation. On the contrary, they should describe their plight in full detail. For their convenience I am, therefore, providing a questionnaire* to which all literate among them should respond informing me about conditions in detail. (My address is: Rev. I.I. Ardan, Olyphant, Pa., Box 418, U.S.A.):

What should the Ukrainians in the Old Country do?

The Old Country Ukrainians should make representation to the (Austrian) Diet or the State Rada, and action should be taken as soon as possible, to induce the Government to organize a bureau of information where people living under the Austro-Hungarian regime, wishing to emigrate, would be able to receive detailed information about the countries to which they may wish to go, and learn precisely what awaits them when they arrive overseas and that the government take action to protect its emigrants against exploitation and deception. Our emigrants have a right to demand this as for generations they have been paying excessive taxes to the Government — money earned with their blood.

In addition to this, it should be in the best interests of a country, that the emigrants would not remember their "old fatherland", as one remembers a mad dog from which he escaped; but, on the contrary, that they go into the world with a feeling that though the "old fatherland" was unable to give them bread, at least it gave them a kind word and good advice.[10]

I.I. Ardan

It was fortunate for the indentured laborers that the American politicians heeded the suggestions of the press that the American governing authorities refused to condone slavery and exploitation. The Ukrainian laborers, on the other hand, by refusing to remain in that state of servitude in Hawaii; by resisting oppression; by taking strike action; and by resorting to other modes

---

* See Appendix.
[10] "Svoboda" No. 6, February 15, 1900. (Translation)

of protest secured freedom not only for themselves, but also for other laborers. *By the Act of Congress that came into effect* the fourth of July, 1900, they (the Ukrainian laborers) became free. Great praise is, therefore, due to the freedom loving American citizens and to the men of the cloth who had the fortitude to help the oppressed, to: Rev. Nestor Dmytriw, Rev. Ahapius Honcharenko, Rabbi M.S. Levy, and above all to Rev. I.I. Ardan.

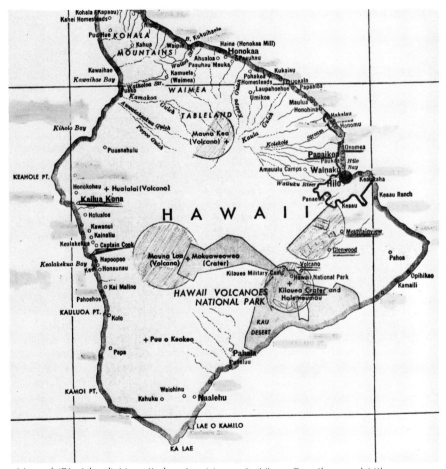

Map of (Big Island) Hawaii showing Mountain View, Papaikou and Hilo areas.

Chapter 9

Dr. Nicholas Russel's Hawaiian Interlude

The precursor of the first large group of Ukrainians to come to Hawaii in 1897 was Dr. Nicholas K. Russel. He preceded that first group by some ten years. Dr. Russel was born Nicholas Konstantinovich Sudzylowsky in Mohyliv in the Kiev area of the Ukraine, on December 3, 1850. He commenced the study of medicine in Kiev, but had to escape from his native land on finding out that he was on the wanted list of the Czar's police — wanted for his liberal political views and for his espousal of the cause of independence of the Ukraine.

On escaping arrest Dr. Russel seemed to follow in the footsteps of Alexander Hetzen and Rev. Ahapius Honcharenko* and reached London. He continued with his medical studies which he completed in Bucharest.[1] Then he left Europe to join Honcharenko in San Francisco where both were actively engaged in organizing a Pan-Slavic society, and in exposing the clandestine activities of the Russian Bishop of Alaska and the Aleutian Islands. This led to Bishop Vladimir's recall!

However, in consequence, the Russian Consul in San Francisco commenced an aggressive campaign to discredit Dr. Russel. Having received an American passport, likely with the help of Rev. Honcharenko, he decided to leave San Francisco for Hawaii.

It appears, that Dr. Russel's close co-operation with Honcharenko ended at this point, though both continued to work to undermine the Russian influence in the Pacific. (Russel, after his contacts with Karl Marx and F. Engels in London) adopted a far more radical approach to the subject of religion and Honcharenko, a clergyman, could not tolerate his radicalism.

In Hawaii Dr. Russel accepted a position as the plantation physician in Waianae on the Island of Oahu and remained there for three years. In 1895 he started a medical practice in Honolulu and, evidently, came in contact with the more important people in the city, among them Robert Louis Stevenson. On learning on the plantation about the exploitation of the native people, he decided to dedicate some of his time toward helping them. As a rule he offered most of them free medical care. During this time, he also was engaged in writing and publishing pamphlets dealing with health, and how to adjust to living in Hawaii. He also took time to visit the other islands and became informed about the needs of the people and the opportunities that were open for the economic development of the Islands.

By the time the first contingent of Ukrainian contact workers reached Hawaii in 1897, he had made arrangements to leave Honolulu.

---

[1] R. Hayashida and D. Kittleson, "The Odyssey of Nicholas Russell":
The American Journal of History, June 11, 1977.
* See Appendix I.

76

Dr. Russel Moved to Hilo in 1897

Of the larger Hawaiian centres he visited, he liked Hilo best and wrote: "It is impossible not to fall in love with Hilo." He also described the Big Island city as a Hawaiian town — much healthier than Honolulu and could be wealthier than the commercial and political centres which had become "too foreign, alien, cluttered and strange."[2] His opinion was that Hilo's wealth lay in its land, that is, "if the government lands upon the neighboring mountain slopes were surveyed, divided into lots and offered for free exchange"[3]. This would attract settlers and develop commerce. He not only wrote about the Hilo area in complimentary language, but he believed in what he said; for in March of that year he acquired a 100-acre tract of land on what they called the Volcano Road, some seventeen miles from Hilo and started to clear his acreage to establish a coffee growing plantation. That same year the Hilo paper reported that Dr. Russel had built a house, erected barns, leveled roads and installed water tanks. The "Hilo Tribune"[4] described him as a "hustler". While he was engaged in developing his plantation, he was engaged in a medical practice in Hilo which necessitated a seventeen mile trip each way, daily. The "Tribune" reported him making another change stating that "Dr. Nicholas Russel, Specialist in eye diseases", established his office on the 17th mile in Olaa, Hawaii.

As Dr. Russel was developing his plantation he was not only taking an active part in the "Coffee Growers Association," but at the same time, he was doing all that he possibly could to help the native Hawaiians in the area. His efforts were also bent on attracting settlers into the area. To help the Hawaiians, and to find a way in bringing settlers, he was of the opinion that it was necessary for him to enter into politics. He was also of the opinion at that time, it seems, that the Big Island of Hawaii, in entering into the American Union, should continue to govern itself as an independent island.[5]

People were beginning to take an active part in politics; in addition to the Republicans and the Democrats, a new party was formed, the Independent Home Rule Party with one, Robert Wilcox, as its head. Robert Wilcox had received some education in Italy and his views were compatible with Russel's radicalism. Though the agents of the Home Rule Party were instructing their followers not to vote for the *haole* candidates; however, with the support of Robert Wilcox, N.K. Russel was nominated and elected to the senate of the Territorial Government.

The first election of the Territorial Government gave the Home Rule Party a majority and the right to form the first administration, and Dr. Russel, no doubt, because he was the man with higher academic preparation was chosen President of the Senate.

As president, this doctor from the Ukraine had some progressive and worthwhile reforms he wished to institute — such as control of alcoholic beverages,

---

[2] Ibid., p. 113 (Stredi, pp. 86-87).

[3] N.K. Russel, "How to Live in Hawaiian Islands", p. 18.

[4] "Hilo Tribune", April 29, 1899.

[5] Ibid., p. 115.

263

LEGISLATURE OF THE TERRITORY OF HAWAII.
SESSION OF 1901.
SENATE.

egan February 20.   Ended May 1.
Sat 58 Days.

N. RUSSELL, President to April 2.
S. E. KAIUE, Vice-President to April 2, President from April 2.
D. KALAUOKALANI, Vice-President from Apri 2.

FIRST DISTRICT.

BROWN, J. T. (I)   PARIS, J. D. (R)
KAOHI, J. B. (I)   RUSSELL, N. (I)

SECOND DISTRICT.

BALDWIN, H. P. (R)   KAIUE, S. E. (I)
WHITE, WM. (I)

THIRD DISTRICT.

ACHI, W. C. (R)   CRABBE, C. L. (R)
BROWN, CECIL (R)   KALAUOKALANI, D. (I)
CARTER, GEO. R. (R)   KANUHA, D. (I)

FOURTH DISTRICT.

KAHILINA, I. H. (I)   NAKAPAAHU, L. (I)
E. CAYPLESS, *Clerk.*

Members of the Hawaiian Senate with Dr. Russel serving as president.
—(State Archives of Hawaii)

land reforms, public health improvements, improvements in public education and the establishment of libraries. He even proposed that a university be organized at Mountain View; and the most progressive idea of his was universal suffrage — giving the women the right to vote.

His progressive proposals did not meet with favor in the senate and the die hards not only opposed him, but attacked him with all their concerted power and with the aid of the press. Since as president he could not propose any of his ideas, he resigned from the presidency, and then in 1902, he did not stand for re-election. Thus ended the political career of the first Ukrainian to be elected to the senate in an American state or territory.

Dr. Russel and the European Settlers for Hawaii

In 1897 when Dr. Russel established his residence in Hilo, on the Big Island, some of the Ukrainian contract workers were employed on the Onomea plantation and others on another plantation close to Papaikou, north of Hilo. He knew of their presence there and was aware, no doubt, that they were experiencing difficulties; however, he neither established close contact with them, nor showed any overt action to assist them. It may be that at that time he was too preoccupied in establishing himself in a new area.

Once Dr. Russel established residence in Olaa, he started to make plans

for the importation of European laborers to the Islands,[6] who would not only meet the urgent labor needs, but in time would become permanent settlers. Earlier he seemed to have established contact with some of his patriots
in San Francisco, and was also in touch with his people in Manchuria, many
of them from the Kiev area where he was born. Before he would take any
concrete action to bring in settlers, he first took steps to see that land be
released in the Olaa forest reserved for freeholders.

It appears that Dr. Russel craved to lead and develop new projects; that
he wanted to establish a sound agricultural base on the Island; and the way
to do this, according to his reasoning, it seems, was to bring European
agriculturists who would be able to establish themselves as successful planters
and whose practices the native Hawaiians could follow to become successful.

Therefore, after discussing his proposals with some of the leaders in his
new, Hilo-Mountain View community, a conclusion was reached that was
desirable to import settlers and to establish agricultural settlements on the
mountain slopes close to Mountain View.

In 1899, therefore, in order to bring this area to the attention of prospective settlers, he wrote an article which was published by "The Hawaiian
Annual," entitled "OLAA". In this article he outlined the physical features,
natural resources and fertility of the soil, also pointing out the opportunities
that existed for coffee and sugar cane growing. He also suggested that the
cultivation of bananas and citrus fruits could be undertaken — stressing that,
in his opinion, it would be to the advantage of the coffee planters to incor-
porate as a joint stock company.[7]

He concluded his article with the following paragraph dealing with the
forest region.

> No wild animals beyond occasional stray goats and horned cattle are met.
> Mongoose and rats do some damage to chickens. Hawaiian born horses and
> cattle do well. Certain breeds of fowl (White Leghorn and Plymouth Rock) do
> well. Of hogs, a mixture of Poland, China and Hawaiian hogs are the best. A
> dozen species of harmless small native singing birds are in the forest. No
> poisonous insects or pests; the jungle is safe as one's own garden.
>
> Dr. N. Russel[8]

In the meantime it was discovered that some birds in the Olaa forest region
were infected with an unknown disease with tumors appearing on their feet
and they subsequently lost one or two toes, "and that several had been shot
which had large tumors around the rictus of the bill."[9] There was no doubt
that people could interpret these tumors as some type of "avian leprosy"
which would eventually be transmitted to other fowl, particularly to chickens,
and in the consumption of chicken meat it could be transmitted to humans.
If the tumors, however, were not a serious infection, it was imperative that
this be investigated to preclude the prospective settlers from rejecting the

[6] Hayashida and Kittelson.
[7] "The Hawaiian Annual", passim pp. 121-26.
[8] Ibid., p. 126.
[9] Ibid.

area for settlement. To have the infection examined by a competent scientist, Dr. Russel was asked to examine the tumors. Then the following report was issued:

> Dr. Nicholas Russel, of Olaa, has kindly examined under the microscope slides made from two specimens, and he pronounces the tumors to be of undoubted bacillic origin.
>
> There is no doubt that the bacilli are derived from the wet bark of trees, and consequently, does not pose any threat to other fowl or humans.[10]

The first announcement he made was the desirability for bringing in settlers from Russia, but mainly from the Ukraine, and Manchuria, which was closer to Hawaii and where there was a large pool of Ukrainian and Russian settlers willing to settle in Hawaii. Before, however, he would undertake to bring in settlers from Manchuria, he considered that it would be much easier to bring a group from the Mainland. His initial effort proved successful and in time two small colonies were formed. We get further information about these colonies from Dr. Russel's letter. He wrote:

> The first and the oldest is located on the 16th mile, one and a half miles from the Volcano Road upon lands that have been free although not reserved. In this colony 400 acres are taken by 5 settlers, 4 houses built and 103 acres of coffee planted. The second, recent, colony on the 22nd mile consists of 5 settlers on 500 acres of the reserved land. So far only 29 acres are planted, but contract is made for 30 acres more to be cleared as soon as the survey is finished.[11]

Some of the immigrants engaged in coffee cultivation (including Dr. Russel) in the Olaa forest region were the following:

V. Elitcheff, 141 acres	N. Russel, 200 acres
C. Slavin, 106 acres	N. Lebedeff, 100 acres
N. Fedoroff, 51 acres	A. Penkovsky, 100 acres
A. Potemkin, 100 acres	N. Muratoff, 100 acres
A. Kraus, 100 acres	E. Yaretsky, 100 acres
M. Komorsky, 100 acres	

We are also provided with more specific information about the first group of immigrants brought to the Big Island by Dr. Russel:

> All colonists belong to the educated class of people: high school teachers, civil engineers, high school graduate boys, army and navy officers in retreat. Three of them are married and have children, the rest are bachelors.[13]

---

[10] Ibid.

[11] L.S. by N.K. Russel to Executive Council (Sic.), Hilo, Hawaii, April 9, 1989.

[12] Hayashida and Kittelson, p. 114.

[13] Russel to Executive Council.

Dr. Russel's coffee-growing immigrants of the Olaa Region. Circa 1900.
—(Bishop Museum)

One wonders whether this group would have the required skills and the desire to toil clearing land and developing the coffee plantations, but according to Michael Lizak,[14] a descendant of the contract workers who came to Hawaii on the Glade in 1898, the colonies were in operation during his time.

However, due to the propaganda waged against Dr. Russel by the Russian officials in San Francisco, he found it difficult to attract many from the Mainland to augment the original numbers. Nevertheless, he was determined to succeed and so turned his attention to the other available sources of settlers: Doukhobors in Europe and Caucasia, the Molokans in the San Francisco and Los Angeles areas, and the peasants from Ukraine, in Manchuria, with whom he maintained contact.

At the time Dr. Russel was pre-occupied in bringing settlers to the Olaa region, the Ukrainians from Western Ukraine were experiencing difficulties as contract workers and seeking help. Though familiar with their plight, Dr. Russel did not appear anxious to champion their cause — probably not wanting to incur the displeasure of the planters whose help and goodwill he needed to get his coffee plantation projects off to a good start. His attitude to contract labor, too, was rather reserved, for as early as 1893 describing plantation labor, he observed, "that Hawaii's contract labor system was not slave labor, but actually provided many benefits for the immigrant workers."[15] Rather a surprising statement to come from one that championed the cause of the oppressed.

Not having much success with getting more of his patriots to come to

---

[14] Michael Lizak in conversation with the writer, Mountain View, Hawaiian Islands, March, 1985.
[15] Hayashida and Kittelson — op. cit., p. 112.

Hawaii, he turned his attention to another group — the Doukhobors. On June 5, 1898 he wrote a letter to President Sanford B. Dole of Honolulu, about the Doukhobors. Referring to Count Leo Tolstoy's letter to the "London times," of September, 1895, he had this to say about the people:

> As with the puritans they are of the highest moral character: total abstainers, vegetarians, frugal, meek class of people, who have made the principle of "non resistance to evil by violence" one of the articles of their creed. Physically they represent the healthiest and most beautiful type of humanity. Economically they all have been, prior to persecution, well-to-do farmers, whose social organization reminds us of the Christian communities of the first century. They call themselves and are generally known under the name of "Douchobertzy", which in literal translation means "Fighter's in Spirit."[16]

Not only did Dr. Russel know about the numbers, 20,000 strong, that could come, but he also knew a less expensive way of bringing them to Hawaii.

> In regard to transportation, I would suggest a much cheaper route than that by which Germans and Poles have been brought here lately. If these dissenters are supplied in the port of Batoum, by which they are ordered to leave with emigrants' tickets on the steamers of the Rusian volunteer fleet to Japan, which, as I am informed, costs but $25., from Japan we could bring them here for an additional $25., so that the whole transportation would amount to $50., instead of $120. as in the case of Germans from Galycia via Hamburg.[17]

The Doukhobor Project

Dr. Russel's project to bring the Doukhobor settlers to the Hawaiian Islands seemed to be stillborn and, consequently, he had to restrict his activities — for the time being — to his coffee growing plantation and to the "Coffee Growers Association." The Doukhobors with Count Leo Tolstoy's[18] blessing, seemed to choose to settle in the Canadian prairies. It appears that the European settlement schemes he proposed which involved some type of co-operative or communal approach were not only incomprehensible to the average Hawaiian businessman and politician, but were also highly suspect. The pragmatic Hawaiian entrepreneur wanted to have nothing to do with settlement schemes which would introduce a degree of socialism into the Islands.

In the meantime, the Ukrainian contract workers, and with them a certain number of Poles, recorded in Hawaii as "Galicians" — their contracts having been cancelled-evinced interest in settling on land in Hawaii. Suddenly Dr. Russel began to focus his attention on these people. As senator, he was eventually "instrumental" in causing a portion of Olaa forest in Hawaii to be opened to settlers,[19] and used his political influence to convince the Government to grant them homestead rights if they would agree

---

[16] Russel to Sanford B. Dole, L.S. June 5, 1898.
[17] Ibid.
[18] George Woodcock, "Canada and the Canadians," Oxford University Press, 1970, p. 88.
[19] Hawaiian Public Archives, Honolulu.

to locate on land as permanent settlers. Since by this time the Ukrainian "contract workers" had been in closer touch with their compatriots in Canada and became better informed that life on the Canadian homesteads was very acceptable, the released laborers concluded that the "homestead plan" in Hawaii, was their new approach to attain a better life in the "Promised Land," but failed to realize and appreciate fully what their lives would be like in the cold damp olia tree jungle, "half way up the Volcano Road near Mountain View."

It has not been possible to find research materials which would indicate precisely the part Dr. Russel played in helping to establish the Olaa forest settlement, after the ex-contract workers began to arrive in Hilo. In 1969, however, an article written by Bob Krauss in the "Honolulu Advertiser" brought his name to the fore again. The article was written as a consequence of a press release by the Russian Novosti Press Agency[20] referring to a book in which one Vladimir Knyp asserted: "Russian Doctor — First President of Hawaii." The assertion was contrary to fact, and Bob Krauss refuted it, and rightly so. Bob Krauss, however, added additional information about Dr. Russel and his plans for the new settlement. He wrote:

> For five years Dr. Russel tried to raise capital for a sugar plantation, but found investors afraid of all sorts of socialistic experiments. He only received testy replies to his letters to Gov. George Carter.[21]

Dr. Nicholas Russel, therefore, failed to organize Ukrainian communities that would function as "Brotherhoods," akin to those practised by the Doukhobors and Molokans. Such schemes were foreign to the understanding of the Ukrainians from the Western Ukraine, and the inflow of immigrants from that area ceased totally. Consequently, Dr. Russel's only hope of establishing any type of Brotherhood in Hawaii that would operate a sugar cane or coffee plantation was to continue with his plans to attract the Molokan group from California and the Ukrainians from Manchuria.

Suddenly there appeared an abrupt change in his activities; leaving his wife on their Hawaiian coffee plantation in Mountain View, he sailed for China in October of 1903, evidently, according to Hayashida and Kittelson, to devote fulltime revolutionary activities most likely among the Russians, and non-Russian Russians in Sibera and Manchuria. What these activities were is unknown; however, the Hawaiian Archives, according to Bob Krauss, are holding his "letter from Shanghai, China, dated February 8, 1904, in which he asks Gov. Carter's help to secure a position for him as U.S. Consul of Manchuria.[22]

There is no doubt that after contacting his Ukrainian compatriots in Shanghai and also the Russian revolutionaries, he was convinced that large numbers of the Manchurian settlers would be most anxious to resettle in

---

[20] See also Iosko, Michail, Mikola Sudzylowsky (1850-1930) v.e. lenina, Minsk, 1976. Library of Congress (call No. C.T. 1218 S877157).

[21] Bob Krauss, "Now Russians Claim the First President of Hawaii," *Honolulu Advertiser*, March 28, 1969.

[22] Bob Krauss, Op. cit. "Honolulu Advertiser".

Hawaii, and that as a Consul he could do much to make suitable arrangments for them. However, receiving neither encouragement, nor serious consideration, he returned to Hawaii after a nine month absence.

Events, however, moved rapidly to satisfy his revolutionary propensity: there was an outbreak of the Russo-Japanese war in the Far East and later from Europe there came news of the 1905 Revolution in Russia. These events made him want to be an active participant in the overthrow of the Czarist Regime, and he soon received an opportunity for at least an indirect initial participation: as thousands of Russian prisoners of war were brought to Japan, and many anti-Romanov activists and leaders of the other nations escaped to China, there seemed to be many liberals among them, and the American war correspondent George Kennan, was of the opinion that there was a need for someone to work amongst these prisoners: to conduct a propaganda amongst them to make them aspire, on their return home, for a liberal government in Russia.

After the Nagasaki Meeting

Dr. N.K. Russel accepted the challenge, went to Japan and worked assiduously among the prisoners of war.* It appears that being so engaged,

Dr. N.K. Russel.

---

* Whether he tried to make arrangements to have the prisoners of war captured by the Japanese released for settlement in Hawaii, is difficult to determine.

he had an opportunity to meet George Kennan in Nagasaki, who described him as follows:

> A well-dressed, courteous gentleman of preposessing appearance, whose speech seemed to indicate that he was an American. I saw at a glance that he was a man of character, cultivation and cosmopolitan experience; but I could not quite understand why an American physician of his age and evident ability should be willing to leave his home and cross the Pacific for the purpose of trying what after all, was only an experiement.[23]

As events show, Dr. Russel paid dearly for his participation in the "experiment" to prepare the interned Russian prisoners to work on their repatriation for the overthrow of the Romanovs. The Russian Government formally protested to the American Government about the anti-Czarist activities of Dr. N.K. Russel, a holder of an American passport — protested against his propaganda activities which, no doubt, not only suggested the establishment of an Independent Ukraine, an Independent Poland and others, but also for the creation of an independent republic formed of Manchuria and Eastern Siberia.

The American Government, without hesitation, seemed to accept the Russian protestations and revoked Dr. Russel's American passport; and it seems, citizenship. Regrettably, it appears, that neither George Kennan nor other liberals on the Mainland, protested against the austere and somewhat cruel action, which made Dr. Russel a refugee for the second time in his life.

After a short sojourn in Japan, where it is reported, he was visited by Sun Yat-Sen, he left for Mindanao, Philippines to practise medicine, thus becoming the first Ukrainian professional to reach the Islands; but not necessarily the first of Ukrainian ethnic group to live in the Islands. He was preceded by T. Kochan.*

Eventually, after some ten years in the Philippines, Dr. Russel moved to China. Though in 1905, he, as liberal, seemed to show some leaning to the Doukhobor tenets, with the loss of his American passport he became more of a radical. It appears that he accepted with extreme disenchantment the fact that a democratic government would accede to the demands of a despotic Russian regime and impose such harsh limitations on a defenceless emigre who had a good record as citizen in Hawaii. He consequently, never returned to live in Hawaii where he left his second wife and the plantation he acquired and developed. After a few years he married a Japanese woman[1] and seemed to settle permanently in Tientsin, China where he died in 1930.

Thus ended the sad odyssey of a Ukrainian "cossack" who came to Hawaii as a refugee and worked assiduously to establish on the Big Island a progressive political and economic structure where the native Hawaiians would progress and prosper and where it would be possible to relocate thousands of Ukrainians from Manchuria and Siberia who were suffering under the repressive Russian overlords.

---

[23] Hayashida and Kittelson, p. 121.

* See Appendix I.

Chapter 10

The Olaa* Forest Settlement

A Ukrainian settlement on the Island of Hawaii was established along a trail which started at Glenwood and ran for about five miles in a north-westerly direction, then after making a turn it joined a wagon road that ran to Mountain View, a small hamlet on the Island of Hawaii, a distance of 10 miles from Glenwood. A few of these settlers were of Polish extraction.

The settlement was established in a manner to replicate a highland Ukrainian village, only that the holdings were larger. The homesteads were located on either side of the trail. However, one may hazard a guess that this settlement looked more like hundreds of settlements established by the Ukrainians who settled earlier in Manchuria around Mukden, in the Ussuri and the Harbin river region, or the Ukrainian villages established in the jungles of Brazil after 1890. The frontage of each homestead was approximately a quarter mile, but much more extensive in depth. In order to reduce isolation engendered by the forest and to provide a modicum of security, the houses of the homesteaders were built — where possible — to face each other.

Bob Krauss reports that: "There were 50-60 families settled in the region along the mountain trail,"[1] but this number may be too high. Others reported the number of settlers at 30-35 families. Each family, evidently received financial assistance "to buy lumber for building a one-room house about 8 by 10 feet."[2] Lillian Shrewsbury-Mesick who lived in the settlement for about a year and a half gives a more detailed description of the houses. It appears that they looked like the shacks the planters provided for their laborers on the plantations.

Mrs. Shrewsbury-Mesick informs us further about the homes of the homesteaders:

> ...Many of these buildings, even when the family consisted of several persons, contained but one room, and that perhaps no larger than eight by eight feet. This one room served as parlor, sleeping-apartment, dining-room, kitchen, bathroom, and store-room when there was anything to store, which was infrequent. Bunks were built one above another in a tier at one side of the room, and if they chanced to be too few or too narrow to accommodate all the family, there was always the floor to "fall back on," though there were times, indeed, when even that was scarcely adequate for the demands upon it. The stove, a table not larger than two by three feet, a small bench that could be hung up when not in use, the bunks and a number of boxes nailed on the walls comprised in many cases the entire furniture of the household. These tiny habitations were

---

[1] Bob Krauss, "Now Russians Claim the First President of Hawaii" Honolulu Advertiser, March 28, 1969, B4.

[2] Ibid.

* Hawaiians now write Olaa thus: Ola'a.

built high from the ground and the shelter thus made under them was used to store wood and whatever else that must be kept dry and could not be placed in the house.[3]

These were not homesteads in the true sense of the word:

The government granted farms, from 50-100 acres in size each, at a cost from $6-$12 an acre (but whose actual value was about $100.) giving the settlers 21 years to pay for them.[4]

Though Shrewsbury-Mesick considered the land in the region as being most fertile, she did not rate the climate in the Olaa region as being typical of the Hawaii climate. She arrived in the settlement late in March of 1905 and stated that, "from late March to early July, the sun shone warm and strong for something less than a day,"[5]. There were long periods of constant "drizzle of rain and the altitude, 2,000-3,000 feet above sea level caused a chilliness that was nearly perpetual and made it necessary for every house to be provided with a wood stove — the fire had to be kept during the greater part of the day and everyone had to keep as close to it as he could get.[6]

In addition to the main settlement of homesteaders, there was a smaller one which, it appears, consisted of a group that was more closely knit through intermarriage, belonged to the Latin Rite and considered themselves Poles. They managed to acquire land closer to Mountain View. It has been possible to find reference to this group's selection of 50-acre lots. The document informs us as follows:

On Thursday, September 20, 1900 at the office of E.D. Baldwin of Hilo, Hawaii, lots located in Olaa, Puna, Hawaii were sold at a public auction and that the members of the former contract working group who arrived in Hawaii on the Glade in 1897 and 1898 acquired lots paying for them more or less $15.00 an acre. These settlers were:

M. Jolkivsky, Lot 45;	Andruch Werbicky, Lot 47;
Michael Pszyk, Lot 46;	Jakub Markewicz, Lot 48;
Jan Larsky, Lot 186;	Peter Markewicz, Lot 187;
and Jan Sajowicz, Lot 195[7]	

The lot numbers suggest that these settlers were clustered close together in the vicinity of Michael Pszyk's farm, and a distance away from the main settlement located on higher land toward the Volcano.

One may readily conclude that the area settled, the climatic conditions and the rain, were not conducive to land clearing — cutting down of olia trees for timber, and the planting of large gardens. What was more: the people did not have draught animals and equipment they could use in the land-clearing operations, and since they needed some income to take care of

---

[3] Lillian Shrewsbury-Mesick, "Paradise of the Pacific," 1912, p. 33.

[4] Julian Bachynsky, op. cit., p. 184.

[5] Op. cit., p. 33.

[6] Ibid.

[7] Report of the Commissioner of Public lands, 1900: Public Lands Notice, pp. 28-31, Olaa, Puna, Hawaii. (Hawaii Archives).

the family needs, the men had no alternative but to go to work in the Mountain View and Glenwood areas. There they were able to earn more due to changed conditions. Consequently, they were able to look for the best paying employment. Much to their satisfactidon, as a result of strike actions taken, the wages on the plantations improved, being raised from $18 to $26 a month. In spite of this they preferred to work building roads: Some worked on the railroad — a line was built for servicing the Olaa plantation area. The building of this railway line (standard gauge — 4 feet 8½ inches) was commenced out of Hilo in 1899, and in 1904 the company extended the line to Mountain View and Glenwood.

To get employment, the men had to be away from home a week at a time, returning to the settlement on weekends only. The task of developing the homesteads, therefore, fell to the lot of the women and children. The Ukrainian women hitched up their skirts and started the inordinate task of rolling back the impenetrable Olaa forest; but with little success. Clearing land of the olia trees which are as hard as steel, was an impossible task. Nevertheless, with the help of the children they managed to plant small vegetable gardens and still smaller flower plots and raised a few chickens.

Children of the Olaa Jungle

The majority of the children who came to the Olaa settlement with their parents were born in Hawaii. Others came to the Pacific Islands around the Horn. When their parents signed the contracts in Bremen and other European seaports, the unscrupulous agents promised the people that a school would be provided for the children. However, this promise did not materialize, and while the parents worked on the plantations — and some of the children soon were of age to earn a few pennies a day — the younger children had no school they could attend and were growing up semi-literate in the "Pacific Paradise," on the fringe of the Olaa rain forest region. The only learning they received was at home from their parents, who found this a most difficult task, as they had no books: Even the prayer books they were bringing with them were hurled into the Atlantic. On the Island of Oahu, a few, however, like the Derko family, were fortunate to be on a plantation where there was a school. But, since the majority of the laborers were Portuguese, they organized a Portuguese school. This school did not give other children much opportunity to learn English — English was the language they needed and wanted to learn.

When the Ukrainian settlers went to their Olaa forest region homesteads in 1900, a promise was also made by the authorities that a school would be built. However, it was built with such alacrity that it did not open until March 20, 1905; in the meantime some of the children were in their adolescence. Nonetheless, when the school opened, the children were most fortunate in the teacher who came out to take charge of the school and to live in the new teacherage that was erected. The teacher was Mrs. Lillian Shrewsbury-Mesick.*

---

* Little is on record about this generous — dedicated teacher, except that she passed away in 1941. (Hilo Public Library).

Mrs. Shrewsbury-Mesick came to the Olaa Forest Ukrainian settlement from Honolulu. She evidently was a jewel of a person and the first bright star in the lives of the people who had, since 1897, lived through the torture of the voyage on the Atlantic, the agony of sailing around the Horn and then the oppressive conditions of life and work on the plantations. Now that they had spent five years of isolation in the forest where their children lived in fear of the forest and some got lost in it, going to school was the highlight of their young lives — a temporary escape from the primitive environment of the Hawaiian jungle.

In spite of the isolation and the lack of contact, the parents, somehow, seemed to have enough time to inculcate in their children the value of education and the importance of school attendance. With a teacher who cared and parents with the right attitudes, the children seldom missed a day of school and saw no reason why there should be such a thing as summer holidays — a time when they stayed at home. And attending school was not easy; very often, with the fathers away at work, the mothers needed their help at home. At times, no doubt, there was a lack of clothing, or even food; they had to wait for the father to return home and bring the much needed supplies, including a bag of flour so that the mother could have bread to make their lunches.*

The children, insufficiently clothed and inadequatley protected from the frequent rains, and with feet unshod, walked, in some instances, miles over a road which was covered with small sharp-pointed stones. Often the feet were raw and bleeding when they reached the school-house and often they were forced to remain at home because of the condition of their feet. This almost broke their hearts, for as a heritage from their parents they seemed intuitively to know the advantages of education, and vacations were, even to the children, a waste of time and opportunity. How they managed to attend school so regularly as they did, hampered as they were by all sorts of adverse conditions, was really surprising. But theirs was the spirit of the pioneer and even the wee ones were infected by it.[7]

It is really incomprehensible how people of this small remote Ukrainian community so far removed from their native land, their ancestral home, their cultural roots; and so isolated in the Olaa Forest on the Island of Hawaii, managed to inculcate in their children the love for better and finer things in life and respect for the opportunities offered. Their children were actually growing up being deprived of things and modes of life so necessary in the normal development of a young mind. They were children who were plunged in the "rain forest zone" where life was as sombre as the weather and the opportunities for a better life nonexistent. It appears rather odd that at this same time that the children of the settlers were suffering severe educational privation, Prof. John Dewey came from the Mainland to Honolulu to expound his theories of progressive education; yet neither he nor his

---

[7] Op. cit., p. 35.

* Mrs. Helen Richardson from Mountain View, some men who worked on the Olaa plantation used to come home on horseback. (The railway from Mountain View to Greenwood was built in 1903).

students knew that in the Olaa forest there were children capable of learning under any method of instruction, provided they were given a chance. However, their teacher knew and cared and their parents, realizing the disadvantages under which their children were growing up, tried to provide some enlightenment using the oral approach and telling and retelling the same old stories, depending, therefore, on the folk-lore and tales learned to enrich the life of the children in the forest community. However, these approaches did not rectify fully the serious cultural deprivation. Mrs. Shrewsbury-Mesick wrote:

> Most of them had seen few books and pictures, and their delight in their schoolbooks and in the few pictures and books I had with me was pathetic. These things opened up a new world to them — a world that had been vague and shadowy. The little stories, so familiar to our own children, were absolutely new and wonderful to them. Santa Claus they had indeed heard of vaguely, but it seemed he had never gotten so far up as the "Ukrainian" Settlement. All the playthings they had were some stick-horses and bundles of rags that might with a great stretch of imagination be conjured to resemble dolls, and their "cows". The cows were twigs from a certain plant whose thorns resemble miniature cows' horns. Tin cans or boxes with bright labels were veritable treasures to them.[8]

Motherless Children

In addition to having to suffer the lack of opportunity to learn, there was a pathetic little family of three motherless little girls and their little brother, Joey. Nothing is known about their mother. She may have been a victim of the Honolulu bubonic plague, or was afflicted with leprosy and taken to Molokai, yet the father, left alone to make a living, and to take care of the children, seemed to have ambitions; he wanted, it seems, to become a coffee grower and, therefore, took a homestead. In the meantime the children had to be fed and clothed, so he, like the other men in the community, had to leave the homestead to find work. The three girls ranging in age from nine to thirteen, beautiful little girls, according to their teacher, and their six-year-old brother, were left to be alone on the homestead:

> The little people — who were but timid children, after all, and afraid not only of the real dangers that might overtake them but a thousand others they could not name, lived alone except for the Saturday nights their father was with them. And these children, except for the few hours' help the tired father could give them after his week's work and the nine-mile walk home, not only kept house, but did their own washing and mending and sewing, raised vegetables, and chickens when the mongoose would permit, baked bread for themselves and their father — and came to school over the sharp-pointed stones! Here was real material for good citizenship. Such qualifications in youth could not but develop into sturdy and honorable characteristics at maturity. They were happy little folks, too, and looked forward joyously to the time when they could "wear sassy clothes and have good eat," as they graphically expressed it.[9]

---

[8] Ibid.
[9] Ibid.

It is doubtful whether those four children would have been able to live alone had it not been for the help and guidance they must have received from the neighboring women. This was one great advantage of a village-type of settlement. It would appear that throughout the week this village in the forest, consisted of women and children only and Mrs. Shrewsbury-Mesick comments on the determination of the women to clear land and grow food stuff..."shivering with insufficient clothing (they) worked like men but could do no more than raise a few vegetables and care for their households."[10] Even the raising of a few chickens was difficult as the mongoose that were imported to exterminate rats, had no desire to do so: extermination of chickens of the homesteaders seemed to be more appealing to them.

The need for warm clothing — a thing hard to imagine in Hawaii — was a serious handicap. Here they could make good use of the warm clothing that was hurled into the ocean, on the instruction of the Captain of the "Glade"—.

Christmas of 1905 in the Olaa Forest Settlement

For years, since their coming to Hawaii, both adults and children alike knew little happiness; however, in 1905 when Christmas arrived, there was a change in atmosphere. The little one-room school became the centre and a beehive of activity; and consequently, the people of the settlement enjoyed a few happy days. This was all due to the attitude, generosity and planning of the teacher, Mrs. Shrewsbury-Mesick. With the help of her kind friends in Honolulu, she was able to see that each child received a Christmas gift; and with the help of the parents and the young people of the community, who worked under her guidance, there was a Christmas tree, a visit from Santa Claus, and refreshments for the children, the young people, parents and the few grandparents.

In the annals of the settlement of the lands, in English speaking countries of the New World, schooling in the remote districts often became the sole responsibility of the teacher, though in some cases the teachers were people rather unprepared academically for the task. In the majority of cases they were people who had the imagination and spirit to do their best and give their all to the community and the children. They wanted to bring happiness and good will. When was there a better time to climax the year's work with a happy celebration than at Christmas? This celebration, as a rule, took the form of a Christmas concert, or in the bringing of a Christmas tree into the classroom; and to enhance the spirit of Christmas, there was a visit from Santa Claus. In 1905 in the Olaa Forest settlement such a celebration took place on the 24th of December. Though the Ukrainian people traditionally celebrated Christmas according to the Julian calendar, and would have wanted this day to be on the 6th of January, they did not object. Besides the 19th of December was St. Nicholas Day for them: and why should not the two be combined? And so it was. So the children enjoyed their first

---

[10] Ibid., p. 35.

Christmas tree in that rural school. They were fortunate to have Mrs. Lillian Shrewsbury-Mesick come to the settlement before Santa Claus.

*   *   *   *   *   *

In the Olaa Forest, in the former Kingdom of Kamehameha, it appeared as if there was a replay of scenes that were resuscitated from the obscure recesses of antiquity and there was a replay of pagan scenes, Druid rituals and the festivities connected with Dazhboh.* There appeared to be a glimmer of the primitive in the forest primeval with the spirits of the ancient Polynesians being revived, too. But these were Christian folk, and for those celebrating Christmas according to the Gregorian calendar, Christmas Eve was the 24th of December. The celebration was carefully scheduled for the 24th which was Sunday and the fathers would be home with their families. This, no doubt, was planned by Mrs. Shrewsbury-Mesick. And what a sacrifice! To bring joy to the community she stayed in the settlement during Christmas Eve and, there being no air transportation in 1905 — she had to be away from her little girl in Honolulu at Christmas.

During the evening of December 23, the Christmas tree, specially selected in the forest, was brought to the schoolhouse, with the parents and the young people helping to trim it, and to deck and festoon the interior as befits the spirit of Christmas. There was also a plan evoked by the school teacher that some young men would run down the trail, and jingle bells, to create the impression that Santa Claus had come to the settlement.

The night of the 23rd of December the interior of the schoolhouse looked beautiful and the people lingered and then they gathered courage and asked the teacher if they may remain longer in the schoolhouse, and sing their Ukrainian Christmas carols; and there in the far flung Pacific Island they broke the silence of the forest, no doubt, with the ever popular "God Eternal is Born" (Boh predvichnyj narodyvsia); "New Joy Has Arrived" (Nova radist stala); and "There Is Good News in Bethlehem Today" (U veflejymi nyni novyna); and others and then they went home.

Once the parents reached home, they likely woke up the children and told them that since they were so far away in the New Country, St. Nicholas could not arrive on the Ukrainian St. Nicholas Day, on the 19th of December, but would likely arrive on the night of the 23rd of December, the day before the Christmas tree celebration, and ride his grey horse through the settlement. And so, along the fern trail of the Olaa forest came the jingle of sleigh bells, and the sleepy children ran out into the clearing around their tiny abodes in the forest and called to St. Nicholas to bring them gifts, and so did Michael Bencharski as he called, "Dear St. Nicholas bring me a knife." But each of the three motherless girls, no doubt, asked for a blue-eyed doll.

*   *   *   *   *   *

---

* Dazhboh — a pagan diety worshipped in antiquity by the pre-Christian tribes of the Ukraine.

Glenwood School.

It was Sunday the 24th of December, and both children and adults came to the schoolhouse. When they entered, the classroom was in darkness, for the windows were covered with bed sheets. Then the candles were lit and began to glitter. The classroom was a veritable fairyland. Things began to happen; presents were given out by Santa Claus, and then:

> The candles on the tree burned low and went out one by one, but no one noticed them, for the boys had their knives in their pockets and were holding each other up at the point of the pistol and firing at Scratchemquick, (the cat), whom they seemed to think had evidently been suddenly transformed into a wild and ferocious tiger that it was necessary to dispatch without delay. And the little girls held their very own precious dollies close to their happy little hearts and beamed on everybody with pardonable maternal pride.

It was a happy evening in the school in the Hawaiian dell and the boys who first of all did not want tops, because they said they did not know how to work them and, therefore, preferred blue-eyed dolls; believed in Santa Claus for the first time.

Then lunch was served to all and to a few of the specially invited — the Hawaiian children. All were happy. The parents in the tradition established in their native land, requested the teacher to ask the children questions to show what they had learned: They were pleased. One of the men stood up, thanked "Mrs. Teacher" and wished her a Merry Christmas.

Chapter 11

The Exodus

Exploited for several years the oppressed Hawaiian sugar cane cutters had had enough of deception and servile treatment. In spite of some seven years of hard toil they failed to improve their economic and social status. Their most important gain was experience. Now that their contracts were abrogated, they started to leave from their Hawaiian entrapment for the Mainland of North America.

However, severing relations with their masters wasn't all that easy for all of them: The planters demanded a "pound of flesh" — full recompense for transportation to Hawaii; payment for goods charged at the company stores; and added to these, fines imposed by the lunas and the planters. Some, therefore, after more than five years of toil, were unable to find enough money to buy their freedom out of the Hawaiian slavery. Fortunately, many of them, however, managed to retain some of the money they had with them when they left their native villages to be able to to pay for their passage from Bremen to Canada; and, with the money from the sale of their patrimony they now were able to buy their freedom. In Hawaii, others had to continue working to save enough to clear themselves of their indebtedness, and pay for their passage out. Those who were able to terminate their employment, immediately left for Vancouver or San Francisco.

There was a small group of European laborers that hated to leave the salubrious climate of Hawaii and decided to remain as free laborers. The planters, too, started to utilize different approaches: They began to offer incentives by providing pay bonuses and other inducements. One of the approaches adopted was to try to keep the different "racial" and ethnic groups apart — to divide and rule:

> On the plantations (the) different racial groups were kept as far apart as possible. They were housed separately, frequently in their individual camps. Racial differences in pay, and opportunities for advancement also preserved this separate identity. Certain groups — the Hawaiians, Puerto Ricans and Portuguese — were given premium status and pay, and consequently remained loyal to the plantation.[1]

This policy of "divide and rule" appeared to be succeeding. In addition opportunities were made available for some laborers to enter into a sharecropping agreement. This further inducement encouraged small groups of Europeans to remain, and the Joseph Bencharskis, who arrived on the "Glade" in 1897, did not leave Hawaii until 1915.[2]

---

[1] Curtis Adler, op. cit., p. 31.
[2] John Bencharski of San Francisco to M. Ewanchuk, August 1984.

Abandoning the Homesteads

On the Big Island in the Olaa Rain Forest region, the homesteaders, after several years of heavy toil under most adverse conditions, became disenchanted. They realized that without heavy equipment they would not be able to roll back the olia-tree forest and become successful coffee growers. They, it seems, came to the conclusion that their homesteads would neither bring them power as land-holding citizens, nor any prosperity within the foreseeable future. The land they held, and the climate in the area, offered them little opportunity to develop into successful agriculturalists. To move and acquire more productive holdings was also an impossibility, for land was not available. To acquire a better appreciation of the situation, it is necessary to review briefly the land tenure on the island of Hawaii.

> In 1848 the Hawaiian King changed land tenure from feudal to private ownership, (and) land holding became consolidated into large blocks and the plantation system was introduced.[3]

As a consequence, there was little opportunity for small holders to acquire land. Land was "locked-up" in the hands of the few who received it in the form of grants, and one large single holder contracted over nine percent of the land the. . .largest 50 land owners (held) 40 percent of the land. Since these landholders were in no way pressured to reduce their holdings, the Ukrainian peasants saw conditions in Hawaii, similar to those that existed in Central Europe during and after the abolishment of serfdom. Consequently, they decided to abandon their homesteads. The time for leaving the Olaa forest region was most propitious: In 1905 there was a considerable out-migration from Hawaii with the Mainland employers recruiting some 11,132 laborers.

On leaving their Olaa forest region homesteads the settlers had no great regrets and most of them were still young enough to "write-off" seven years of life in Hawaii as a bad experience. They took to the wagon road, and family after family trudged its way through the dells to Glenwood, and then reached Hilo. The mothers and fathers were leaving the thresholds of their homes for the second time — never to return neither to their native Ukrainian homes nor the settlers' abodes in the Hawaiian forest.

However, the children left the forest region with regrets. Those who passed by the school that stood empty and silent in the dell recalled their one most happy year in a classroom with one of the finest teachers, Mrs. Shrewsburry-Mesick. In the annals of the Island of Hawaii, she, no doubt, deserves to be recorded as one of the most benevolent, gentle and dedicated pioneer teachers, who brought joy to the children, some who came to Hawaii from Ukraine, and others, like little Joey, who were Hawaii-born.

The Olaa Forest settlers in abandoning their homesteads, little realized that had they only had the resources to cut the olia trees and sell them, they could have become well-established. No one, however, informed them

---
[3] Op. Cit.

about the value of those trees. History, therefore, seems to repeat itself, and for the second time in the history of the Hawaiian Islands, Europeans left natural resources that could have made them prosperous: the Ukrainian settlers left the olia tree forests; earlier Dr. Schaffer left a fortune in sandalwood in Kauai.

By 1906 many of the contract workers had adjusted to the life in Hawaii and a small number decided to remain there permanently. Some acquired better land, and others secured employment and thus a small community was established in the Mountain View area.

Mrs. Lillian Shrewsbury-Mesick's Postscript

Seven years after the memorable Christmas concert in the Ukrainian settlement in the Glenwood school, Mrs. Shrewsbury-Mesick returned to the colony she penned these nostalgic reminiscences in the "Paradise of the Pacific":

> This was seven years ago. The schoolhouse never held another Christmas tree for before another holiday season had come the "Ukrainians" had given up their brave but heart-breaking struggle and had left their holdings. The radiant roses they planted wherever there was room still bloom, fragrant and beautiful. The birds sing as they did at dawn and twilight when we lived among them. But the "Ukrainian" no longer comes over the fern-trail on Saturday nights to bring his scant store of supplies and spend a few hours with his family.

Exodus to the Mainland

The majority of the contract workers of 1897-98 on leaving Hawaii left for San Francisco, while others went to Canada. By this time many of them had acquired acceptable knowledge of the English language, and the Hawaiian misery had served them as a good "school of life" — they learned to adjust to new conditions. When they arrived in San Francisco, they were free men and there were no restrictions on them in applying for available work. They soon established contact with their San Francisco compatriots — Hawaiian refugees; those who came to Hawaii in 1897 on a three-year contract were able to leave for San Francisco earlier. The majority of homesteaders of the Olaa Forest region who did not want to remain in Hawaii were, therefore, the last large group to reach San Francisco.

The San Francisco Experience

As each small or larger group of the former contract laborers arrived in San Francisco, they, no doubt, tried to establish contact with Rev. Ahapius Honcharenko — the man who did much to help them secure release from their contracts. Honcharenko* was then living in Hayward, California, on

---

* See Appendix I.

his farm he called "Ukraina", but the aged pilgrim was not in a position to provide help or leadership to the Hawaiian emigres. All he could offer them was a Sunday church service in his chapel, in a cave, baptize their children, or marry young couples.

By the time, the Hawaiians began to arrive in San Francisco, the members of the "Ukrainian Brotherhood of California" who could help them were dispersed. M.I. Stechishin, Yurko Syrotiuk, and Iwan Danylchuk returned to Canada.[4] For a while Stechishin worked in a saw mill in Nanaimo and was active in the socialists groups in the Vancouver area, and he later became one of the better known journalists among the Ukrainians. T.D. Ferley who did not come to Canada until 1907, became actively involved in politics and was the first of his group to be elected to the Manitoba Legislature. Stechishin, after publishing a socialist paper, "Robochy Narod" in Winnipeg, in spite of the influence that Van Dyke and Jack London, both Honcharenko's friends, had on his socialist ideals, left the socialists before World War I.[*] George Syrotiuk remained in Vancouver where he was engaged variously as a real estate agent and vendor of farm produce. Most of the leading activists were, therefore, gone from San Francisco.

The new contingent of laborers from Hawaii were not impressed with Honcharenko's "Ukraina", nor with the Sunday service in his Cave. They investigated possibilities of settling in Castro Valley as a group, but found land around San Francisco too expensive. Soon many left for Canada and other points in U.S.A. Others found climatic conditions acceptable, and being tired of roaming, decided to remain in San Francisco. In their group there were tradesmen and artisans who found very satisfactory employment at wages four to five times higher than the few cents they earned as sugar cane cutters.

The Great Disaster — San Francisco Earthquake

It appears, however, that as fortune would have it, arriving in San Francisco did not spell the end of their misery, for as more laborers were arriving — particularly the homesteaders of the Olaa Forest region — they were greeted by yet another disaster: In March of 1906 the City was struck by an earthquake. They feared the havoc like that caused by the volcanos, and the tidal waves in the Hilo area. There was great destruction of buildings and other property, fires raged and there were 400 dead. Whether any of the new arrivals were lost in the earthquake, is not known. The earthquake, however, only created a temporary setback for the new arrivals. As a consequence of the "great disaster" work became available for all: first in the clearing of debris, and then in the rebuilding of the city; those who had no definite settlement plans in mind decided to stay and thus formed a part of a permanent Ukrainian colony in San Francisco.

---

[4] S.P. Symchych et al., "British Columbia and the Ukrainians, 1927-1957, Vancouver, B.C. Passim, pp. 20-36.

[*] John London abandoned socialism about the same time.

Hawaiian Refugees in San Francisco

Thus far it has not been possible to get information about the people who remained in San Francisco. We know that D. Puchalsky who worked hard to secure the abrogation of the contracts remained. Mr. Andrew Sarokowski, a San Francisco attorney, writes as follows:

> I have made an inquiry with Mr. Stanley Hlynsky who is 87 and came to San Francisco in the early 1920's. He says that some Ukrainians did indeed come to San Francisco from Hawaii. One was named Puchalsky; he belonged to the local "Prosvita" and had a shoe store in the Portola District. (His two daughters Millie and Julia evidently still live in San Francisco.)[5]

Then John J. Bencharski writes to say:

> From the information I received from my parents, it appears that my father came to Hawaii as a contract laborer in 1897. He left from the German port of Bremen, travelling around the Horn, disembarking from the vessel, H.F. Glade, on July 27, 1897. My mother arrived at the same time. She came to Hawaii with her mother. On arrival in Honolulu my parents, though both only seventeen years old, were married at Tenchupu and my father went to work on the sugar cane plantation. Their children John, Peter and Helen were born in Hawaii and in 1915 they came to San Francisco, where the other three children, Micheal, Frank and Thomas were born. The Micheal to whom you refer as being among the homesteaders in the Olaa Forest, was my father's brother who also came to Hawaii at the same time. In Hawaii, it seems that my father worked for several years on the plantation as timekeeper.
>
> When we came to San Francisco, my father first worked for several years for the American Can Co., as a machinist, and then until 1952 he worked at the Pacific Freight Yards. He died in 1952, and my mother in 1971. The house where we lived still stands, but has new owners. Life for us children was good in San Francisco. We got good jobs and lived a good life.[6] All the children got married; I have been married to the same woman for 52 years. We own our own home and are now both retired. With the exception of my youngest brother Thomas, my sister and all my brothers have passed away. Thomas is now 62 and I am 82 years old.

Mrs. Derko of Alberta

For an example of the families who went directly from Honolulu to Canada, we depend on the information provided by Mrs. Derko of Alberta. She, as a young girl, arrived in Hawaii with her parents, who belonged to the second group of Ukrainian contract workers to come to the Islands. In the record of her reminiscences there is a brief reference to her life in Hawaii. We learn from her that she attended school and learned Portuguese. Her father worked with Japanese and Portuguese laborers. Though Mrs. Derko

---

[5] Letter sent by Andrew Sarokowski to M. Ewanchuk, July 6, 1983.

[6] L.S. by John Joseph Bencharski of San Francisco to M. Ewanchuk, of Winnipeg, August 6, 1984.

liked Hawaii, her parents were very lonely and were most anxious to join their relatives in Canada who wrote and told them that "they owned many acres of land."

Mrs. Derko's father worked to the end of his five-year contract and then leaving the other eight families of his group, left for Alberta. Her description of their arrival in Edmonton is interesting.

> We arrived in Canada at the end of March, 1903. We had sailed across the Pacific to Vancouver and from there we went by rail to Calgary and Edmonton. We got off the train in Strathcona. We arrived in light summer clothes because there's no winter in Hawaii, and we were greeted in Edmonton to such a blizzard that we couldn't stand outside the station for a minute. My father immediately ran to find a store with winter clothing for us. Otherwise we would have frozen to death. Luckily, he still had some money left. We cried and complained that father had taken us away from Hawaii to this Siberia. Had we known that Canada would welcome us the way it did we'd never have moved from Hawaii, because it's a paradise compared to Canada. It's always warm.[7]

From Hawaii, the Land of the Nene*, to Goose Lake Manitoba

---

[7] William A. Chumer, "Recollections About the Life of the First Ukrainian Settlers in Canada", (L.T. Laychuk, translation), Canadian Institute of Ukrainian Studies, Edmonton, 1981, p. 24.
* Nene - Hawaiian national bird.

The Yakimishyn family had the advantage of being together on the plantation at Papaikou, so when their contracts were abrogated, the male members of the family unit which included the Fitkalos and the Bidochkas went to work on the railroad track where they were able to earn better money, and after a while were able to leave Hawaii for the Mainland. They arrived in San Francisco where they received employment, and in the meantime, Panko Yakimishyn left for Canada to examine homestead opportunities in the Ethelbert, Manitoba area where his son, Peter, lived on a homestead, and he, himself, selected a homestead close to the place that Yurko Syrotiuk first settled.

At that time a new railway line was being extended west from Dauphin through Gilbert Plains, Grandview on to Goose Lake (now Roblin). The region north of Goose Lake was hilly, the soil was sandy and drainage better. They, therefore, decided to locate there and trekked west along a new grade made ready for the laying of steel. They took up homesteads north of Goose Lake, in an area that probably reminded the Hawaiian immigrants from Papaikou of the glens and dells of the Olaa Forest region, between Mountain View and Glenwood, where they worked building a railroad bed. Consequently, when they organized a school district, it was named Gleneden. They liked the new area much better and encouraged their relatives and countrymen to join them.

In time the Kuluks and the Stybas arrived to resettle north of Goose Lake; then they were joined by Panko's son, Nykola who had had enough of the Brazilian jungle and came to join them.[8] They built a fine Ukrainian Catholic church, a community hall for cultural and social activities and were able to be in touch with people of their ethnic group. Ukrainian newspapers they could read were available and the isolation they experienced in Hawaii did not exist.

After the Syrotiuks and the Yakimishyn group left San Francisco for Canada, others followed to settle in Vancouver. Among these were the three Dolawrak brothers, I. Korbutiak, Iwan Dragan, and Hryhory Kraykiwsky. Hryhory Butenko, who, it seems, knew Dr. N.K. Russel, after a short sojourn in Vancouver left for Shanghai, China. Some years later, during a political campaign, Panko Yakimishyn was pleasantly surprised to be able to renew acquaintance with T.D. Ferley whom he first met in San Francisco. It is interesting that while Yakimishyn came from the village of Kossow in Western Ukraine, T.D. Ferley came from the highland area close to a renowned village of Kosiw.[9]

The Yakimishyn group did well in Canada. They had to work hard as farmers, their descendants as farmers, businessmen and people in the professions made good progress. There were three Yakimishyn sisters in the service of the Ukrainian Catholic Church as nuns, one clergyman, several teachers, one school administrator and a computer specialist who has a masters degree and started postgraduate work toward a doctorate; one school

[8] Interview with Wasyl Yakimishyn of Roblin, Manitoba, grandson of Panko and from his letter to M. Ewanchuk, October 2, 1983.

[9] S.P. Symchych et al., op. cit. passim.

teacher is married to an Orthodox clergyman, and one grandson was an artist.

There are many who went to Hawaii who have relatives and people from the same villages in Canada. Mrs. Rose (Mrs. Peter) Kondra recalls her grandmother, Mrs. Frank Zubrak, telling her that when she came to Canada, people from her village of Bileypotik went to Hawaii. Very likely they were the Gabriel Mochnacz family.

It is difficult to trace all those who left Hawaii and came to Canada — many stayed in the U.S.A. However, Paul Nimchuk, whose parents settled in Hazelridge area of Manitoba thinks that the Nimchuks from the village of Dzhuryn may have been relations.

A Mr. Kolomyja formerly of St. Martin and now of Winnipeg, came from the same village of Kotsubyntsyki, as the Mykola and Maria Kolomyjas and their four children (18, 14, 12 and 9) who went to Hawaii in 1898.

There were Stogryns in Hawaii, Micheal and Tomko, and there is a Stogryn in Illinois. Many, however, lost contact with their relatives and countrymen.

Though many people from the Slobidka village went to Hawaii, others came to Canada and some settled in the St. Norbert* area of Manitoba.

From Hawaii to Rat Portage*

Yakim Knysz, was an adventurous soul; in 1898 he left his wife and children in the village of Verbovets in the Western Ukraine and was on his way to select a homestead in Canada. In Bremen, however, like hundreds of others, he was talked into going to Hawaii to work on sugar cane plantations. He signed a five-year contract and sailed with the rest of his countrymen for the Pacific Islands.

Hawaiian employment, however, being unsatisfactory, Yakim Knysz, after he worked out his contract decided to return home to the Ukraine, but chose to travel through Canada stopping in Rat Portage where some of his countrymen were living. After working for some six months cutting pulp wood, (instead of sugar cane) he returned to Verbovets.

In the Ukraine he found living conditions unsatisfactory: there was no employment, and much worse — no freedom. He and his wife Katherine, therefore, disposed of their property and taking their three children, a girl and two boys, came to Canada and settled permanently in Kenora, Ontario. He, however, did not advise friends to go to Hawaii to work. On October 17, 1921, Yakim Knysz became a Canadian citizen. His children and grandchildren have done well in Canada. Yakim Knysz is one of many thousands of Ukrainians who made a great personal sacrifice in life to be able to establish a better future for their descendants[10] in the New World.

---

* According to David A Lenchyshyn, his grandfather and father came from Slobidka.
* Now Kenora, Ontario.
[10] Information provided by Frank A. Dubenski of Winnipeg, grandson of Yakim Knysz.

King Kamehameha the Great.

PART II

Harbin
to
Honolulu

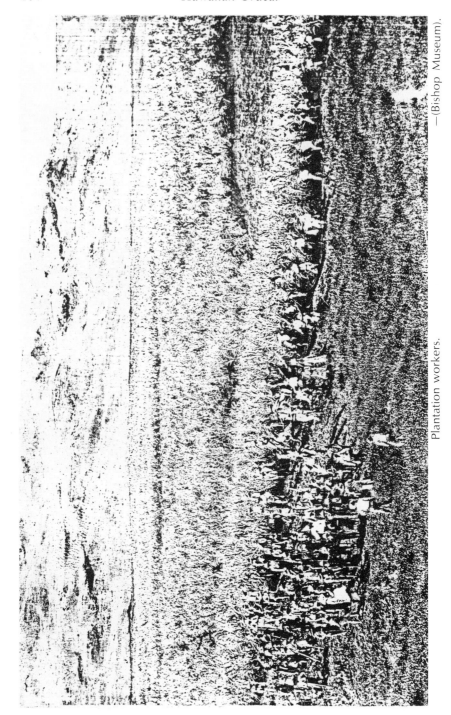

Plantation workers.

—(Bishop Museum).

Chapter 12

Further Search for European Labor
Labor Supply on the Decrease

After the abrogation of contracts of the Ukrainian groups of 1897-99, the numbers of these workers decreased in a substantial degree, and the recruitment of other Europeans reached a low ebb. In addition to the departure of the Ukrainians, there was a significant out-migration of other laborers — "Caucasian laborers"[1] as they were then called — to the American west-coast cities. The Hawaiian Board of Immigration and the Planters' Association were in a dilemma fearing that with this exodus there would develop a preponderance of Japanese in the Islands. The Planters' Association, consequently, alerted its agents to commence recruiting European labor from any sources that were available. Among the agents, no doubt, there were some of the former acquaintances of Dr. Russel, notably Atkinson and Perelstrous. They proposed an idea of exploiting Dr. Russel's suggestions of bringing to Hawaii people from areas under the control of Imperial Russia, among them those who were seeking religious freedom. Time for such action was particularly opportune as the Board of Immigration[2] had a large fund available for extensive recruiting activities of labor.

The Molokans

However, they soon found out that the Doukhobors recommended by Dr. N.K. Russel were no longer available as they had, in the meantime, established settlements in Western Canada. However, there were smaller religious groups of Molokans*, who left Russia and came to the areas around Los Angeles and San Francisco. There they found it difficult to acquire land as it was too expensive. They, therefore, were available as settlers and laborers in Hawaii. In 1906, with the assistance of Samuel Johnson who acted as an interpreter, it was possible to attract a group of Molokans to Kauai; and in 1907, agents of a German sugar company brought another group after promising them an opportunity to settle on land but, when the Molokans arrived in Honolulu, they were informed that there was no land available for them. The company explained that they had merely been hired for work on the plantations.[3] And again we see deception and falsity in practice.

The Molokans as "Spiritual Christians of the Sect Jumpers," however, refused to work in the Hawaiian swamps cutting sugar cane for a pittance, when they could earn $2.00 and $2.50 a day in the Los Angeles area. Complaints

---

[1] Herman, Bernhard L., "The Caucasian Minority", Social Progress in Hawaii, Vol. XIV, pp. 38-50.

[2] Appendix to Board of Immigration Report of 1909-1913, p. 4.

* See Appendix I.

[3] McLaren, N.A. quoting: Peter A. Speak "A Stake in the Land", New York, 1921, p. 29.

were made and an investigating committee was sent to Kauai. They were: Revs. O.H. Gulick, J.M. Lydgate, J.W. Wadman, D. Scuddes, and Mr. J.M. Martin.[4] The four clergymen reported that the land holding Molokans were most satisfied with their arrangements in Kauai; they were, however, misinformed for the people soon gave up their holdings — each family losing on the average of $1,000.00, joined the laboring group, and all returned to Honolulu to wait a boat that would take them to the Mainland. The planters, therefore, recorded another failure, but seemed unperturbed and sought an alternative. They then accepted the second of the two proposals made originally by Dr. N.K. Russel: the recruitment of Ukrainians and other ethnic groups, in Manchuria where the people were brought by the Russian government from their fertile chernozem holdings in the Ukraine, to settle in the Manchurian taiga. As the two agents, Perelstrous and Atkinson, knew the language of the people and also were acquainted with the Manchurian areas, they were engaged for the new project. No effort, however, was made to seek direct assistance from Dr. Russel, who at that time was living in Japan or China.

The Perelstrous — Atkinson Project

Once the planters demonstrated interest and provided financial assistance for the importation of laborers from Manchuria, Perelstrous and Atkinson took immediate action. They planned their campaign carefully and well. First, they advertised in the Harbin paper in Manchuria published in Russian, outlining settlement and labor opportunities in Hawaii, and when they received some inquiries they took the next step; prepared a pamphlet to assist them with the project. The pamphlet was carefully planned and edited to make it possible for the average reader to understand the contents. The material was presented in question-answer form. This twelve page pamphlet, "Hawaiian Islands", priced at 20 kopeks, was written in Russian by no other than A.H. Perelstrous, and published in Vladivostok by a printer, V.K. Johansson.[5]

In translation the first page of the Perelstrous' pamphlet reads as follows:

> *Brief Description of Hawaiian Islands* followed by statement of purpose:
>
> I shall try (in this pamphlet) to reply to every question that may be of interest to the people wishing to move with their families to live in the Islands.

Q: **How much land will each family be able to acquire from the plantation companies, and who will be entitled to acquire land, that is, may a family — if it wishes — acquire land for ownership?**

A: From 10 to 25 acres.

---

[4] "The Friend", oldest newspaper west of the Rockies, no. 5, Honolulu, May 1906, pp. 5-6.
[5] National Archives, Washington, D.C.

Гавайскіе Острова.

Цѣна 20 коп.

А. В. ПЕРЕЛЬСТРУЗЪ.

ВЛАДИВОСТОКЪ.

Типографія В. К. Іогансонъ.

Recruitment Pamphlet on Hawaii
—(National Archives Washington, D.C.)

Q: **What is the cost per acre?**
A: From 50 to 150 rubles depending on the quality of the soil.

Q: **How much can a newly arrived family that is unable, or does not want to engage in agriculture earn a month?**
A: One is always able to get employment doing day work, and, at the present time, a man may earn from 40-45 rubles a month. There is a need at the present time for laborers on plantations, and this work can guarantee a man to earn the same amount.

I ought to observe: if laborers will remain working steadily on a plantation, they will be able to live in one of the wooden houses belonging to the planter. The dwelling, therefore, will be closer to his work and enable the women and girls to work, and earn from 20-22 rubles a month, and 14 year old boys earn from 32-36 rubles a month. However, according to the American Law, children younger than 14 years are not permitted to work for wages. For better clarity I ought to say, that the law in the Hawaiian Territories makes it compulsory for children of all nationalities in the age group of 6 to 14 years attend school, but when they reach 14 years their parents are under no obligation to keep them in school.

The pamphlet further informed the readers that in the American schools children received instruction in all subjects in English only; that all schools were public schools, which were free — and all parents had to provide was books, exercise books and slates. Additional information was as follows:

–   Men may also work on coffee plantations. The work there is neat and clean and they pay $1.00 a bag. A man may pick 3 - 3½ bags a day and a woman can pick 2 - 3 bags. Children may also do some picking. (The size of the bag is not stipulated.)

–   Artisans and mechanics earn more than laborers.

–   Crops grow well. An acre produces 40 - 50 tonnes of sugar cane; and 2½ - 3 tonnes of coffee. Pineapples yield maybe, 8 - 10 tonnes, an acre. Hemp is also grown. Coffee, however, needs constant cultivation, but after the shrub is two years old it is tilled and pigs may keep the weeds down.

–   Hauling sugar cane is hard work and requires stronger men who may earn $2.00 a day.

–   Portuguese and Japanese people who live on the Islands cultivate from 10 - 20 acres of sugar cane.

In reply to the question: "How much a family that received a free house, fuel and water can earn in a month?" Perelstrous informs his reader:

–   For a 10 hour day, and working a 26 day month, a family with two sons and a daughter working may earn 120 rubles in addition to a free 2 - 3 room house and free medicine and medical care.

Picture of a house a laborer was to live in.

— The median temperature in Hawaii is 27° C with a high of 32° and a low of 25°.

— People are able to buy their provisions in the plantation stores. Credit is available.

— Cost of food and materials:*

flour	2 rubles for 50 lbs.
rice	8 rubles for 100 lbs.
pork	30 kopeks a lb.
beef	20 kopeks a lb.
eggs	5 kopek for a group(?)
chicken	1½ - 2 rubles
duck	30-60 kopeks
fresh fish	10 - 12 kopeks a lb.
beans	5 - 9 rubles for 100 lbs.

— The main port to which produce is exported is San Francisco, which is some 2,000 nautical miles away. It takes six days and nights to reach it. Vladivostok is 4,000 nautical miles away and requires a 20-day trip. This includes all transfers.

---

* Note:

[1] 100 kopeks were equal to a ruble; a ruble equalled half a dollar.

[2] The pamphlet used English weights, and Russian currency. Not using metric terms confused the laborer.

[3] The Ukrainians have a term for a period of time of one day and one night, "doba". In Russian it is called "sutka".

[4] In land measure, Perelstrous did not use the term hectares; but acres.

Chapter 13

Manchurians Show Interest in Hawaii

The Perelstrous pamphlet was widely circulated among the laborers and the villagers of Manchuria — and widely read. Hawaii, therefore, the peasants thought, presented them with a window through which they would be able to see and finally attain the benefits of the democratic system of government. With the promise of schools and the learning of the English language, Hawaii, to the agriculturists, seemed to be a land of better opportunity for their children; to the political activists, Hawaii spelled freedom from oppression and a better life for all, and better conditions in the workplace.

The information and arguments advanced by Perelstrous in his pamphlet impressed the Ukrainian people and other Europeans, then living in Manchuria, and many showed interest in moving to Hawaii. They were, also, no doubt, attracted there by the good climate, an opportunity to acquire land and the chance of getting out of Manchuria and the oppression imposed on them by the Russian officials.

The relocated settlers of the Siberian-Pacific area were anxious to cast off the yoke of the Romanovs, much more so after 1867 when the refugee Ukrainian clergyman, Ahapius Honcharenko commenced publishing his "Alaska Herald" in San Francisco, in which he suggested that a new republic be created of the Ussuri and the Amur river regions and the territory of Alaska, and that the area be known as the Republic of Ukraine. The Ukrainians living in Mukden, Harbin, Vladivostok and Blahovischensk, consequently, believed that this would in time take place, but in the meantime they craved an opportunity to escape from the control of the Russian administrators. In 1870 the "Alaska Herald", therefore, formed a new link of communication between Harbin and San Francisco, where, in time, colonies of immigrants from Russia became established.

As a consequence of the interest created by the Perelstrous pamphlet, he and Atkinson were invited to come to Harbin to explain labor and settlement opportunities in Hawaii.

Consequently, the first party recruited from the village of Alexiev arrived in Honolulu from Vladivostok by the vessel "Siberia" in October, 1909.[1] Since it took about six weeks to reach Honolulu from Harbin, the laborers must have left Harbin on or about the 15th of September, 1909, and started to make preparations to leave during the spring of 1909. The Perelstrous' pamphlet, therefore, must have reached the Amur and the Ussuri colonies in 1908; and plans for contacting the people in Manchuria must have been started after Dr. Russel left Mountain View, and the Ukrainian settlers abandoned their homesteads in the Olaa Rain Forest region.

---

[1] Testimony of Anton Shustakewitch of Olaa Plantation, National Archives, Washington, D.C.

Laborers from Manchuria Arrive in Hawaii

The first group to arrive in Hawaii from Manchuria on October 21, 1909, consisted of 157 men, 66 women, and 80 children. Twelve of this group were detained in Japan and arrived later.

On arrival they were checked and passed as being physically fit, by the Inspector Brown, assisted by Samuel Johnson who acted as interpreter. All signed for plantation work and were dispatched to Olaa and Waiokea on the Big Island; Kahalui, Maui; and Makaweli in Kauai. The cost of bringing in these laborers was nearly $17,000 (of the $86,000 available for the Manchurian project) which included over $1,000 for A.L.C. Atkinson's salary and an undisclosed amount paid to A.H. Perelstrous[2] for his efforts and expenses.

The sending of the laborers to the Big Island seemed a wise one. On the Olaa plantation were some of the settlers who left their Olaa forest homesteads, working as laborers and lunas, and were in the position to give the newly-arrived laborers much of the needed guidance. The planters in Olaa, Kahalui and Makaweli, it appears, were highly pleased with the new group of laborers, and considered them highly desirable. They, consequently, asked for more people of the same class of laborers.

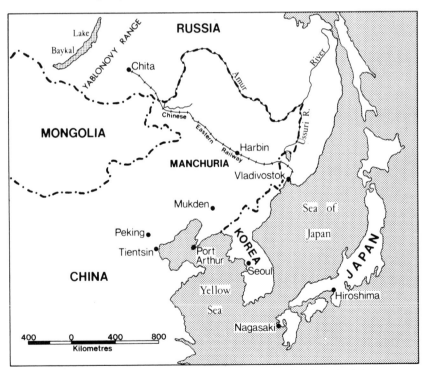

Map of Manchuria showing some centres settled by Ukrainians.

[2] Nancy McLaren, passim pp. 43-44.

Old Siberia - A street in Chita.

Guards (in black) and prison labor in Siberia (W.H. Jackson) (Courtesy Emil Lengyel, *Siberia*).

The Japanese Intervention

Before the laborers from Harbin arrived in Honolulu, the Japanese contract workers on some plantations went on strike demanding higher wages. There was dissatisfaction among the Japanese, too, that according to the 1907 "Gentlemen's Agreement" the number of contract laborers to be recruited in Japan was to be substantially decreased. This new arrangement was put into practice in order to appease the Hawaiian "haoles" who were insisting on limiting the number of Asiatics brought into the country, and who were well pleased with the well-built Europeans that were brought into the Islands.

In the meantime, however, a report appeared in the "Japan Weekly Gazette"[3] alleging that the new laborers recruited (and some twenty-five thousand available) by Atkinson were not Russians, but Galyaks, an Asiatic tribe. This report threw the Hawaiian haoles in consternation and suggestions were made that the Manchurian project should be stopped. The situation became acute enough and Perelstrous was asked to clarity the matter.

Ukrainians not Russians

Perelstrous who came to Hawaii from Vladisvostok knew the territory and the settlers in Manchuria, he, consequently, made a very satisfactory explanation: He announced that it was true that the new laborers were not Russians, but they they were Europeans; nevertheless, however, not Galyaks. He stated that the new laborers were a totally separate ethnic group from the Russians called "Little Russians" by the Moscovites; they were Ukrainians from the Kiev* and Poltava** and Don regions of the Ukraine.

As the planters continued to be satisfied with the new laborers, they accepted Perelstrous' explanation, and asked for more of the same ethnic group. As a consequence, Perelstrous and Atkinson immediately left for Manchuria for a large-scale recruitment campaign.

Laborers Dissatisfied

Although a period of twelve years had elapsed from the coming, in 1897, of the Ukrainians to Hawaii, conditions of work for the contract workers had changed little. Work was demanding and rigorous, and in some regions, particularly the Big Island, the rains made life miserable. Moreover, the land that was promised to the Ukrainian settlers was not available; they had to buy their clothing and produce in the company stores where there was little choice and things were more expensive. On some plantations they had to work long hours and were driven by merciless lunas who, though they may have refrained from using the cow-whip, used other approaches in making the people work harder.

One other factor that frustrated the laborers was the fact that they lacked

---

the knowledge of English and could not communicate with the planters and the officials. Perelstrous had promised that they would be given a teacher, and be able to attend school. None of these promises were kept. They, consequently, complained and wrote to him early in 1910. They received this reply:

Honolulu, 23rd of May, 1910

Mr. Katspshak
Dear Sir:
I received your letter and can tell you that I think there has been some misunderstanding between you and your plantation office because you have nobody who knows the English language and therefore you could not make yourself understood. I would be very glad to help you but I am busy in town at present. The last party of Russians will arrive here in three weeks and at that time I will go to every island and will help everybody to explain all the misunderstandings.

I learned that very many people like to have a Russian-English dictionary and ordered therefore several hundred copies. To be able to send these books to those parties who want a copy kindly let me know if you or your friends wish to have one, send me the names of the families in particular and I will mail the dictionaries through your plantation office, which is to receive the money for the books. I cannot tell you how much these books will cost but I think only a very small amount.

Most respectfully
A. Perelstrous[4]

The Perelstrous letter in response to the request made by the laborers was, as may be seen, very non-commital. He was not prepared to accept any responsibility and treated the whole matter as a "misunderstanding." When the laborers appealed to their bosses, that they be given a teacher of English, they felt that the intention of the planters was to keep them ignorant so they would refrain from making demands. The planters also were trying to intimidate the workers.

One group reported:

When we asked them to give us a teacher of the English language, they gave us the straight answer that for that very reason one of the Russians has been arrested on the Makaweli Plantation.[5]

The planter, no doubt, wanted the people to reach the conclusion: "If you continue with your demands, you may also land in prison."

Nevertheless, dissatisfaction among the laborers was setting in, particularly when they found out that the laborers who refused to work on plantations and took employment in Honolulu were making good money. Most of them, therefore, had their minds set on going to Honolulu and from there to San Francisco. And when they discovered that their status as contract workers

---

[4] A. Perelstrous to Katspshak, (translated from Russian) National Archives, Washington, D.C.
[5] Ibid.

made it possible for them to go to the Mainland of the United Stated — their minds were made up. At one plantation in Kauai, the laborers simply packed up and came to Honolulu to catch the first boat for the United States.

Although there was no word from Manchuria for several months, the report from the planters was that their "enthusiasm for the laborers from Manchuria already in Hawaii did not flag. True, there were a few minor disturbances due to language difficulty, and confusion about wages had arisen, but those were settled amicably."

Dr. N.K. Russel with family and friends in China. (Courtesy Iosko, Mikhail).

Chapter 14

Recruitment of the Second Group of Laborers

It was much easier for Atkinson and Perelstrous to recruit the second group of laborers in Manchuria. When they arrived in Harbin, they found that their pamphlet had done effective work: It was widely read and by many settlers who were induced to leave the Kiev, Poltava, Odessa and the Don regions of the Ukraine. They were lured by the extravagant promises made to them by the Russian officials about life in the "Far East". When they arrived in Manchuria and took up land in the Ussuri and the Amur river regions, to their chagrin, they found isolation and geographic conditions difficult. Therefore, on finding that the first group had arrived safely in Hawaii, many of them were prepared to leave and were expecting the agents to come to their region so that they could sign agreements to go to the "Paradise Islands."

There is no doubt that the Russian officials were also interested in reducing the numbers of disaffected Cossack peasants who had always resisted being governed by the Russians. This would make it easier to keep in control the population far removed from the centre of government.

On arriving in Harbin, however, Perelstrous and Atkinson found out that they did not have to go into the more remote regions to recruit the Ukrainians, "Little Russians", as requested by the Board of Governors and the Planters' Association. They found out that in the larger centres, particularly Harbin, there was an adequate supply of laborers from which they could select the best applicants for Hawaii. During the winter months, as employment on the building of the Trans-Siberian Railway stopped, the unemployed laborers flocked into Harbin. All of these were not necessarily Ukrainians, they, however, were ready to go to Hawaii so they could eventually reach the Mainland of the United States. The attitude of these unemployed laborers who had just been released from the oppressive tactics of the overseers, could not be rated as being very amenable to similar working conditions in Hawaii.

In Harbin and Vladivostok there were a number of prisoners of war who — after being released from the Japanese prisons — chose not to return to Europe but remained in the "Far East". They, no doubt, had, to a degree, fallen under the influence of Dr. Russel's propaganda about the need to overthrow the decadent Romanovs, and now that they had a chance to leave, decided to do so; they, too, were less disposed to tolerate any oppressive tactics. Added to these groups, were the released political prisoners from the Siberian jails — many of them intelligent men — who fearing that their attitude to the authorities in the "Far East" may again land them in the Siberian prisons, were most anxious to leave. They, however — more than the other people recruited — were opposed to any type of oppression and exploitation; be it Russian or that of any other government.

117

The recruitment situation being most favorable, Atkinson and Perelstrous did not have much difficulty in signing up their quota of laborers, and felt that they could easily attract twenty-five thousand. Perelstrous was even more optimistic: He knew the disposition of the abused subjects of the Czar and was of the opinion that 100,000 was a figure that could be attained without difficulty, and this, of course, would satisfy the Hawaiian entrepreneurs for it would ensure the white's man dominance in Hawaii.

The two agents, it would appear, were not concerned that they did not recruit the group requested, and felt, no doubt, that the new group would make a rapid adjustment to conditions of life and work. When the vessel "Siberia" docked in Honolulu there was a total of 300 laborers ready to debark.

First Problems with the New Group

It would appear that problems with the new group arose early. The laborers left Harbin and Vladivostok during the winter season and were clad in heavy and warm, Siberian type of clothing, and, when the vessel began to sail in warm seas, as they approached Hawaii, they were most uncomfortable but had no other clothing to wear. This, no doubt, put them in a very unfavorable frame of mind, their mood changed for the worse, and they became agitated as they reached Hawaii.

On arrival in Honolulu, on the 17 of February, the laborers — after being detained in port for a couple of days — were examined on the wharf and then post-haste were taken to the sheds to be divided into groups and dispatched to the different islands — and different plantations. As they were not permitted to go into Honolulu, they became suspicious, and when they found out that some people of the October group were in Honolulu, insisted in contacting them.

However, though strict measures were taken to prevent any contact, the Manchurians managed to do so, and they found out from the first group that they were deceived, that the promises were not kept, and that the working conditions were horrendous. Consequently, the newly-arrived immigrants promptly began to make demands for firm assurances: They made it clear that unless they were allowed to see the plantations, where they were to work, they would not move off the wharf.

Diphtheria and Measles

While the laborers were showing opposition to being hurriedly moved out of the port, a serious problem developed: Several cases of measles and diphtheria were found among the immigrants; all had to be placed in quarantine and transferred to the Quarantine Island. To add to an already tense situation another group of over a hundred arrived. These laborers did not quite understand why they, too, were placed in quarantine, yet there was no one who could act as interpreter, to provide them with an explanation. Fortunately, there was a "singer" in town who was Russian or knew Rus-

Laborers from Manchuria lived in Camp Iwelei close to the wharf in Honolulu while on strike.

—(National Archives, Washington.)

sian, and she was asked to explain the situation to the immigrant laborers. Eva, as she was called, acquitted herself well and the immigrants began to appreciate their position better.

However, when the quarantine was lifted and the laborers were ordered to go to work, they refused to comply with the directive and remained on the wharf where a food supply was not available and sanitation was inadequate. Nevertheless, they refused to go to work until such time that the complaints raised by the first group were rectified. By March 4, it was found that four hundred of the group had to be requarantined; three days later another group of 249 arrived on the boat "Korea", and the authorities had to bear the cost of providing medical care for a large number of people; about fifteen had to be hospitalized.

Manchurians Go To Work

Eventually when the epidemic at the port of entry subsided, and the quarantine was lifted, the laborers decided to go to work and were taken to various plantations on the Island of Oahu and others. Conditions on plantations remained unchanged, and three months later the laborers, after making a good effort to succeed decided to go on strike. The press, however, reported that they revolted.

> After three months of suffering and quiet submission, having spent not only their scant earnings, but the money they brought with them, realized from the sale of their real property and other belongings at home, the men revolted; they left the plantations and went to Honolulu, with a view of informing the American Government, through its regularly constituted authorities.

> The people looked for work elsewhere, but could find none. The Government of the Territory was informed, by a delegation sent by the men of the unbearable conditions, but the only answer that they received from the governor was that

they were to return to the plantations, and a promise to improve the conditions of their life was made.

The people returned to work, but found no fulfillment of any of the promises made, and the people began to appeal for assistance from the outside world.[1]

Not all the laborers, however, returned to work, and those who remained on strike were driven out of their miserable shanties and their belongings were strewn over the open fields. The strikers were left "homeless and breadless". They could not get work of any kind for the planters and other employers closed ranks and would not hire them. Many had no money left and had to depend on their compatriots for financial assistance. In order to gain help from other sources, the whole group in Honolulu decided to send a delegation to the President. They managed to collect enough money among themselves to pay for the transportation of two men.

Delegates Go To The Mainland

The "Washington Times" provides us with additional information about the sequence of events that followed:

They have sent two delegates to go to Washington; on their way these delegates stopped at the imperial Russian consulate at San Francisco, and there they were assured by the consul that there was no necessity for them to go to Washington, advising them to return to Honolulu. The consul having referred them to a Russian representative, one Kerberg, who, he assured them, would take care of their grievances and remedy all wrongs.[2]

In visiting the "imperial consulate" the group of laborers made the same error the first Ukrainian group of 1897 did when they appealed to the Austrian consul (Hackfeld) in Honolulu, and he instead of helping the aggrieved had orders issued to have them arrested. In the case of the Manchurian group, de Kerberg came to Hawaii — and after making a very cursory investigation of conditions in the Honolulu area — was interviewed by a reporter of a Honolulu paper, "The Pacific Commercial Advertiser", which immediately published in bold type, the following front-page news item:

Russian Government Agent Tells His Countrymen They Should Go To Work[3]

Adding: and "tells them not to expect any aid from him". He further stated that he had visited the Ewa and the Waialua plantations and, that the laborers at work on these plantations, appeared to be well off and satisfied except

[1] "Washington Times", Saturday, July 2, 1910. National Archives and Records Service, Washington, D.C.
[2] Ibid.
[3] "The Pacific Commercial Advertiser", Vol. II, No. 8635.

that they wanted night schools at which they could learn the English language.[4] The report in the "Advertiser" carried further information that was far from sympathetic to the maligned laborers.

> I told the leaders. . .that they need not expect the slightest pecuniary aid from me, and that I would not aid people who didn't work. . .It seems to me that they should go to work on the best conditions to be had here, and I told them so. . . For example, the statement that they understood until they came here that a ruble was equal to a dollar is absurd. They had changed their money before coming here, and they must have known about the difference in value.[5]

It is true that the immigrants knew that they could earn 45 rubles by working on the plantations, but since they only learned about the exchange value of a ruble in terms of the American dollar when they were on board the vessel that was transporting them to Honolulu, it was too late to do anything about it. They had reached the "point of no return."

From the report in the "Advertiser", it appears that de Kerberg's remarks did not help the striking laborers in the least; in fact, it gave them bad press and severe condemnation from an agent representing the country from which they came.

On the other hand the visit by the agent from the Russian consulate appears to have been most helpful to the planters: He seemed to provide guidance to them how to treat the strikers — Russian style. He labelled the striking workers as idlers and stressed the fact that among them there were many radicals; that their leaders were socialists and anarchists. He, no doubt, may have suggested that the Russian mode of approach of bludgeoning the strikers into submission be utilized; that the leaders be arrested; and that they and the laborers be threatened with deportation. It appears crystal clear that de Kerberg's visit did not in any manner ameliorate the distress of the strikers, but acerbated it.

Those of the strikers who were of Ukrainian extraction understood why de Kerberg would refuse to help them, but there were also many who were Russians and had hoped that de Kerberg would understand their difficulties and plead their cause. The strikers were, therefore, embittered and enraged and, no doubt, cast some aspersions on the "sukinsin" de Kerberg. Whether they threatened to shoot him, as the planters claimed, is not certain; from the laborers' point of view, no doubt, such action was justifiable.

The planters soon came to the conclusion that some of the leaders of the group, and also some of the laborers that were on strike, should be deported. On the other hand the American immigration officials in Hawaii who were abreast with the situation did not consider that such a drastic action was necessary. The acting Inspector in Charge of Immigration discouraged such action and informed his office in Washington that although the men refused to work on the plantations, they, however, were prepared to accept

---

[4] Ibid.
[5] Ibid.

employment at the wharf in Pearl Harbor.[6]

He also pointed out that the people on strike were prepared to accept privations and some had worked and lived on white bread until such time as they could earn enough money to go to the coast, adding:[7]

> There was something more than hysteria over labor agitators that led to the unusual efforts to induce them to go to plantations. . .
>
> The unwillingness to work as contemplated on plantations was due to the fact that the first were sent, with little ceremony, to where they had no land to give them and the disappointment in other respects was too much for them.

He concluded:

> Matters will work out without the immigrants becoming public charges here — I am of the opinion that deportation for other cause than physical disability will not be necessary.[8]

Map of Ukraine showing districts from which Ukrainians emigrated to Manchuria.

[6,7,8] Passim. Reply of Richard L. Halsey, letter No. 52986/i-o to Commissioner General of Immigration.

Chapter 15

Strikers' March in Honolulu

Not being able to garner even a modicum of support from any source,
placed the striking laborers in a distressing situation: No church, no welfare
organization, and no governmental official made any effort to assist them.
The men and women who faced many privations on their way to the "New
Land", the country between the Amur and the Ussuri rivers — to be away
as far as possible from the juggernaut of the Russian officials — on coming
to Hawaii found themselves under the heels of the planters and their sadistic
lunas. The only hope left for them was to make their way across the Pacific
to San Francisco. The prime objective of the planters, on the other hand,
was to have the contract laborers carry out the spirit of the contract and
perform their tasks as directed to the fullest degree possible — to cultivate
their plantations and harvest their crops at the lowest possible cost. They
wanted to recover the advance made toward the cost of transportation incurred in bringing the laborers from Harbin to Honolulu.

Each new group that arrived was prevented from going to Honolulu. The
fear was that the new laborers would establish contact with agitators. And
the Hawaiian press seemed to give some credence to the fact that the
agitators were undermining the program started by Atkinson and Perelstrous.
We read in the Hawaiian paper an article to that effect:

> That outside agencies are at work and undermining the Russian immigration
> scheme is alleged by some who have the best interest of the movement at heart.
> When the Russians were at Kobe, a Russian agent went among them and poured
> tales into their ears designed to make them dissatisfied with conditions here.
> It is said that Vasiliev held a long conference with this agent, and ever since
> he has been regarded as an agitator, and it is due to him that the last overture
> of the Governor and his confreres failed to take root among the immigrants.[1]

Consequently, when the strikers continued to be adamant about not returning to work, the authorities acted: They arrested three of the ringleaders,
H. Vasiliev, Biloff and Surupov; charged them with vagrancy and sentenced them to three months in jail.

The arrest of the three was the most disturbing happening to the immigrants
in Hawaii. They were of the opinion that the three would be deported to
Siberia, where they would face many years of incarceration. They, therefore,
showed a strong bond of solidarity among themselves and began to make
plans to stage a protest, asking for the release of the three; and the only
action they could take was to march to the prison and ask for the recon-
sideration of the heavy penalties imposed.

News of the intended march reached the police and, they, fearing that
there may be an attempt by the marchers to free Vasiliev forcefully, got

[1] Washington Times, July 1910.

somewhat agitated, and as a consequence the Chief of Police gave orders to his men that if the marchers attempted any such action, "to shoot to kill"; action was also taken to reinforce the police station.

The marchers left camp and in due time gathered at the police station.

> Word reached the police station about half-past five o'clock that the Russians had left their camp and that they were marching in a body toward the town. Sherriff Jarrett had just returned from a funeral as the Russians assembled at the police station. The Sherriff saw at a glance that serious trouble was in sight, and he attempted to parlay with the Russians: Jarrett's object was to delay action as long as possible till a bicycle officer could be sent around and call the police officers off their city beats.

> The foot police on the city beat only amounted to four men, but they were hurried in to the rescue. Counting the Sherriff, there were only a half dozen men at the police station. The Sherriff called upon the trustees to come out and they were quickly given clubs with which to disperse the mob. The Russians had all gathered outside the station and were demanding to see Vasiliev, who was confined inside. Jarrett ordered the mob to disperse but not a move was made by the Russians, who only yelled louder.[2]

From this press report, it appears that though the strikers may have caused some anxiety to the authorities, and created considerable commotion asking for the release of Vasiliev, they definitely did not resort to any violence. There was, therefore, no need for the pressing of the trustees into police service and arming the untrained men with clubs — men, many of them very likely capable of mayhem. When the marchers, on being ordered, failed to disperse, men, women and children were attacked in a most brutal manner and yet the reporter of the "Advertiser" seemed to imply that the marchers were cowardly:

> The big hulking Russians grabbed their children and held them up as shields with which to block the blows of the clubs and "billies". The mounted men did good work in dispersing the mob and within a few minutes of the start of the police charge there was not a Russian — except those in the cells — near the police station.[3]

The end result of the episode was that the marchers were dispersed. Ten men were arrested and six of these received prison terms of six months. Many women returning to their camp became sick and some, it was reported, miscarried before they reached their miserable shacks.

Fearing further reprisals and finding themselves in dire straights — not having means of feeding their families — some men returned to work on the plantations.

The laborers, no doubt, felt that the public of Honolulu was against them and that their only solution was to earn money to be able to leave for San Francisco. To these exiles from Russian bondage, as to the groups of 1897-98 — Hawaii instead of being a "New Jerusalem" turned out to be "Hell".

---

[2] "Advertiser", p. 2.
[3] Ibid.

Chapter 16

A.F. of L. Takes Action

Unsatisfactory conditions of work and living were driving out laborers who were imported from Manchuria to the Mainland — laborers that were able and competent. The wooden-headed attitude of the planters who resisted change were also creating dissatisfaction among those who remained. Of course, only those could leave the Islands who had enough money to pay for their transportation and Head Tax from Honolulu to San Francisco — a considerable number did have enough money; and they left. When they arrived in San Francisco they informed members of the labor groups about the plight of their countrymen in Hawaiian servitude. In time the information reached the leaders of the organized labor group in New York and their president took action. On June 9, 1910 he wrote a letter to the Department of Commerce and Labor. Receiving no reply he made a press release, and as a consequence on Saturday, July 2, 1910, the "Washington Times"[1] published a report that peasants from Hawaii were held in peonage:

Slavery in Hawaii is Gomper's Charge

Department of Commerce and Labor is asked to Investigate

Miserable Conditions Depicted in Memorial Presented by A.F. of L. Head

Conditions akin to slavery in the Hawaiian Islands are pictured in a memorial by Samuel Gompers, President of the Federation of Labor to the Department of Commerce and Labor.

Sugar planters, acting through the Hawaiian Government, Gompers charges, have been luring peasants from Harbin in the interior of Siberia to the Islands. Russian and Hawaiian agents are engaged in the work.

They recruit peasants, Gompers says, by attractive pamphlets and in these and by other means promising the peasants wages of $45. a month, free houses, fuel, electric lights, furniture and an acre of land each for gardens, evening schools, free hospitals, half pay during sickness, free railroad fares and free schools for children.

A delegation of 300 deluded Siberians went to the Islands last October, and the total number that yielded to the lure of the sugar planters is over 1,000.

---

[1] National Archives, Washington, D.C. July 2, 1910.

Worker from Manchuria going to the plantation. Showing houses lived in by a family with two little girls.
—(Ray Jerome Baker, Bishop Museum)

Shows house, fuel and running water as promised.
—(Ray Jerome Baker, Bishop Museum)

The people did not find the comforts claimed, not homes advertised but wooden shacks without roofs and floors. No fuel was provided and the men had to bring sugar cane roots, coal is a luxury and seldom obtainable. There is no electricity. There is no free transportation to work and men have to walk a long distance, if they arrive late by five or ten minutes they are punished with a quarter-day deduction in pay. The wages are $22. for men and $13. for women.

After three months of suffering and quiet submission, having spent not only their scant earnings, but the money brought with them, realized from the sale of their real property and other belongings at home, the men revolted: they left the plantations and went to Honolulu with a view of informing the American Government through its regularly constituted authorities.

The people looked for work elsewhere, but could find none.

The governor of the Territory was informed by the delegation sent by the men of the unbearable conditions, but the only answer that they received from the governor that they were to return to the plantations, and a promise to improve the conditions of their life was made.

The people returned to work, found no fulfillment of any of the promises made, and the people began to appeal for assistance from the outside world.

Laborer with baby, 1910.   Mother and baby.
                                                —(Bishop Museum)

The two column eight inch news item brought the Hawaiian labor situation in the open. Following the "Washington Times" report, President Samuel Gompers wrote another letter[2] to the Hon. Charles Nagle:

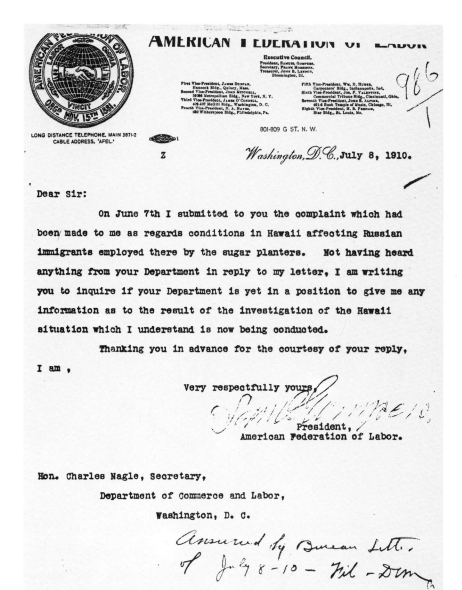

AMERICAN FEDERATION OF LABOR

Executive Council.

President, SAMUEL GOMPERS.
Secretary, FRANK MORRISON.
Treasurer, JOHN B. LENNON,
Bloomington, Ill.

First Vice-President, JAMES DUNCAN,
Hancock Bldg., Quincy, Mass.
Second Vice-President, JOHN MITCHELL,
10306 Metropolitan Bldg., New York, N. Y.
Third Vice-President, JAMES O'CONNELL,
402-407 McGill Bldg., Washington, D. C.
Fourth Vice-President, D. A. HAYES,
500 Witherspoon Bldg., Philadelphia, Pa.

Fifth Vice-President, WM. D. HUBER,
Carpenters' Bldg., Indianapolis, Ind.
Sixth Vice-President, JOS. F. VALENTINE,
Commercial Tribune Bldg., Cincinnati, Ohio.
Seventh Vice-President, JOHN R. ALPINE,
401-6 Bush Temple of Music, Chicago, Ill.
Eighth Vice-President, H. B. PERHAM,
Star Bldg., St. Louis, Mo.

LONG DISTANCE TELEPHONE, MAIN 3871-2
CABLE ADDRESS, 'AFEL.'

801-809 G ST. N. W.

Z

Washington, D.C., July 8, 1910.

Dear Sir:

On June 7th I submitted to you the complaint which had been made to me as regards conditions in Hawaii affecting Russian immigrants employed there by the sugar planters. Not having heard anything from your Department in reply to my letter, I am writing you to inquire if your Department is yet in a position to give me any information as to the result of the investigation of the Hawaii situation which I understand is now being conducted.

Thanking you in advance for the courtesy of your reply,

I am ,

Very respectfully yours,

President,
American Federation of Labor.

Hon. Charles Nagle, Secretary,

Department of Commerce and Labor,

Washington, D. C.

Answered by Bureau Lttr. of July 8-10 - Fil - DUM

---

[2] Gompers to Nagle, National Archives Washington, D.C.

On July 9, 1910 Secretary Nagle[3] received a gift of nine resolutions from the 'Hawaiian Labor Defence Conference'' and a covering letter:

NICHOLAS ALEINIKOFF,
93 NASSAU ST., N. Y. CITY
SECRETARY

DR. JULIUS HALPERN,
51 EAST 91ST STREET,
TREASURER

July 9th 1910.

Hon. Charles Nagel,

　　Secretary, Dept. of Commerce and Labor.

Sir:-

　　Pursuant to the instructions of the citizens of New York, in mass meeting assembled on Union Square last night, we beg to enclose copy of the Resolutions unanimously passed at the meeting.

　　That the demands of American organized labor and the prayers of liberty loving citizens of the United States will be fully and favorably considered by your Department, is the sincere belief and trust of

　　　　　　　Very Respectfully Yours,

　　　　　　　Hawaiian Labor Defense Conference,

　　　　　　　　　　Secretary.

Two of the resolutions and the preamble read as follows:

The appalling state of affairs existing on our Territory of the Hawaiian Islands has revealed to us:

That our alien contract law, as passed by Congress of the United States, has been continuously and systematically violated by the sugar planters of the Hawaiian Islands, acting through and under cover of the Territorial Board of Immigration, and a state of peonage is fully established and maintained on the territory of the United States, is a violation of law.

Resolution no. 9 seemed to summarize the feelings of the labor group the situation of the striking laborers in Hawaii.

---

[3] Nicholas Aleinikoff to Hon. Charles Nagle, Secretary, Department of Commerce and Labor, July 9, 1910. National Archives, Washington, D.C.

That notwithstanding the most brutal treatment, coercion, intimidation, and imprisonment, there are at present about 600 of these laborers men, women and children roving on the coast and through the streets of Honolulu, homeless and breadless, preferring death by starvation to slavery in the sugar plantations.

Both President Gompers', and the Defense Conference's letters were acknowledged, but no indication was given as to what investigative action was contemplated. Nevertheless, the governmental authorities finally did take action and had the complaints investigated. The newly organized A.F. of L. and their president, therefore, saw that they met with success in entering into a labor dispute — their first — in Hawaii.

Samuel Gompers.
—The Globe and Mail, 20 Apr. 1984

Chapter 17

Investigation by Immigration Officials

Eventually the Secretary of Commerce took action and appointed Mr. R. Brown, Inspector-in-Charge to investigate the problems that developed with the laborers brought in from Harbin. Working with him was the Commissioner-General from the Bureau of Immigration and Naturalization, Danl. J. Keefe. To carry out the investigation the Inspector divided the new immigrants into two groups, and those wanting to leave for San Francisco were invited first.

Testimony of San Francisco Bound Group

Credit is due to the two officials for conducting the investigation in a responsible manner. The laborers called to testify were first sworn in by the Inspector-in-Charge, Mr. Raymond Brown, and were then questioned by Mr. D.J. Keefe. The questions ("Q") and answers ("A") were recorded. From these testimonies we were able to gather the following information:

Testimony of Nikifor Bashnino:

Mr. Keefe: What is your name?
    A: Nikifor Bashnino.

    Q: **How old are you?**
    A: Forty-one.

    Q: **Have you a family?**
    A: Yes, myself and wife.

His wife, Marva, according to the testimony, was 41 years old also. They had been in Hawaii for eleven months, coming there from Harbin. The couple had about 70 rubles when they left Harbin and arrived in Honolulu with 25 rubles. Their fare to Hawaii was paid by Atkinson and Mr. Perelstrous.

    Q: **What have you been doing here since you arrived here?**
    A: I did not go to the plantation. I have been working here in town. I have been working sometime at the station, then on the wharf, and sometime in the pineapple factory.

Mr. Bashnino stated that he did not work for two months after his arrival. He tried to get work, but, "they laughed at us"

Q: When you took passage at Harbin didn't you understand that you were to go to work on the sugar plantation?

A: Yes, I could have gotten work, but we sent ten of our people to go and look into the conditions on the plantation and they came back and said it was not good and so we did not go.

The Bashninos left Harbin on the 3rd day of January, 1910, and arrived in Honolulu on the 15th day of February on the steamer "Mongolia". After he received work he earned $1.50 a day but did not work steadily, only about 10 days a month and earned $80 in ten months.*

Q: How much did you earn while in the Islands?

A: I only figure the money that is left. The money I spent for my living, I don't know how much that is. Sometimes it costs about twenty-five cents or thirty cents for one day to live.

Q: What do you expect to do in San Francisco?

A: My friend wrote me (about four weeks ago) and told me they need railroad laborers.

Mr. Keefe:

There is no demand for laborers in San Francisco now. A great many men are out of employment and the number is increasing every day. Under these conditions you are making a very great mistake in attempting to go to San Francisco at this time.

A: It is all the same, I want to go.[1]

Michael Tsybish:

A twenty-nine-year-old man when interviewed by Mr. Keefe testified that he came to Hawaii from Harbin. He had forty-two rubles and forty-two kopeks, about $21.00 American when he left, but arrived in Honolulu with only ten rubles or $5.00. On arrival he was placed in quarantine for three days and then marched to the planters' shed where he remained for a day, but was refused permission to go downtown. From the shed he was placed on a steamer and taken to the Makaweli plantation on the Island of Kauai. After three months there he left and sailed to the Island of Hawaii where he worked at the Waiakea plantation until he came to Honolulu. For some time in Honolulu he could not get employment. Finally getting work "digging ditches for sewers." At the time of the interview he was penniless, having spent his last quarter for a meal that day.

Q: How are you going to get to San Francisco?

A: I cannot go without money.

Q: What is your purpose here?

---

* It would appear that the investigation took place in mid-December, 1910.

[1] National Archives and Records Service Bureau of Immigration and Records, Naturalization testimony, Washington, D.C., pp. 9-13.

In reply Michael Tsybish stated that he came to Honolulu as a member of a committee of three to deliver a petition to Mr. Keefe.[2]

Iustafia Kalashnikov Testimony:

Mr. Kalashnikov, age 38, arrived in Hawaii on March 22, 1910 with his wife and six children aged 13, 12, 11, 8, 7 and 2, and when interviewed had fifty dollars left. They arrived with thirty dollars and lived in camp Il-awaii for four weeks, and were likely among the group that was beaten and dispersed by the police and trustees. Working in Koloa, Kaui, he made $25, and his wife $14, and one boy, $6.00. "Some months I would have $5.00 left and some months I would not have anything." He worked nearly every day, but had to stay home sometimes to get a rest.

The family plan was that he go to San Francisco first by himself and leave the family in Hawaii with $20.00, expecting the people to help his family if the need should arise.

> **Q:** **Why are you going? You could get employment here.**
> **A:** What is the use of working here if I can get nothing for my work. I can hardly live on what I am earning here.

After their experiences on the Hawaii plantations, the immigrants became more bold and were not afraid to speak out. Of course, they could do so knowing that the American interviewing officials were gentlemen and did

Women forced to work like men carrying sugar cane up the gangplank when loading cane.

—(Bishop Museum)

---

[2] Ibid. pp. 14-16.
[3] Ibid., pp. 17-20.

not use the knout like the Russians were apt to do. Even women were not afraid to testify and demonstrated a tendency to be outspoken. This may be detected in **Minna Tatiana's testimony:**

By Mr. Keefe:

Q: **What is your name?**
A: Minna Tatiana.

Q: **Where are you going?**
A: To San Francisco.

Q: **Are you a married woman?**
A: Yes.

Q: **Have you a family?**
A: One girl.

Q: **Where is your husband?**
A: He is here, sitting down.
(Witness is withdrawn and husband put on the stand.)[4]

There is no doubt that the immigrants did fear deportation and, therefore, may have been of the opinion that the sooner they get out of Hawaii, the less chance there would be of being deported to Siberia.

Testimonies of Those Unable to Leave for San Francisco

Having received the testimonies of the San Francisco bound group, the immigration officials in charge of the investigation recorded the testimonies of those who wanted to leave but lacked the financial means to do so.

Stephen Soloviov, Wailua, Maui

Q: **Who asked you to come here?**
A: Mr. Perelstrous and Mr. Atkinson.

Q: **Have you found the conditions here just as they were represented by these two men?**
A: I have not found what I was told.

Q: **What did they tell you?**
A: A man could get a piece of land and if he could not buy a house, the plantation would buy it for him.

Q: **Do you consider your condition here worse, equal, or better than in Manchuria?**
A: I am living worse. . .I may find a better place, I don't know.

Q: **Are you satisfied to stay here?**
A: If they pay me a good salary and give me a house, yes.

---

[4] Ibid., p. 21.

Q: **What do you consider a good salary?**
A: $1.70 day. Now I don't get enough to pay for my living.

Q: ·   **If you had to do it again, would you leave Manchuria for Hawaii?**
A: No. I have had enough of it.

Q: **Would you rather go back. . .than stay here at your present wage?**
A: I can't answer that.

Kyrylo Pipko, plantation laborer, age 35, wife and four children testified that in Hawaii he had to work almost for nothing, complaining also that the house promised the immigrants was not made available. And though promised that they could work almost anywhere, found out that the only work he can get is work on the plantation.

> They said we would get 45 rubles a month and after working for three years we would have a house and one acre of land all our own. After three years if we wanted to sell the place, the plantation would pay us $300.00 for the house and land. They said that if we didn't want to work on the plantations we could work other places or plant corn or anything we wanted to do. Here it seems to be all cane.

In response to the question whether he considered his condition better in Hawaii than in "Manchuria", Mr. Pipko's reply was:

> "I have been here for a year and I have no money for my daughter to buy books to go to school and I have been working every day. If I should get sick, what would my children do?"

Three single men testified, and when asked why they came to Hawaii, Peter Nazarenko replied: "I was asked to come here and it didn't cost anything," and Alex Kostiv and Gregor Horlic responded: "We were not satisfied (here), but we have no other place to go." Kostiv also complained that they had no opportunity to learn English.

Testimony of Anton Shustakewitch of Olaa Plantation:

Anton Shustakewitch, age 52, wife and six children, came to Hawaii with the first party from Harbin in October, 1909 and liked Hawaii, but they were not getting what they were promised. Though the manager has given the family an acre of land, he is not keeping the promise to provide electric lights and an eight-hour work day. As a fireman on the railway he was earning good money in Manchuria, but since his party was not told the relative purchasing value of the ruble and the dollar and, now the family finds that it is impossible to get along on the wages they receive.

The interviewer on investigating the Shustakewitch account in the store, appended the following note to the testimony:

> (By reference in the store books, I find that the last man, Anton Shustakewitch, had a bill of $15.00 charged to him at the plantation store during the month of July and he earned $15.20 in the same month.)

Q: Has the plantation offered you any land?
A: Yes, Mr. Perelstrous told us we would have land.

Q: Have they given it to you?
A: Our house is in the forest and the land is not good for growing anything.

Likely a Shustakewitch house.

Chapter 18

Labor Protests Continue

Before the investigators could reach all the plantations on the other Islands, complaints began to arrive from there which indicated that the situation on plantations in Kauai, Oahu, Molokai and the Big Island were the same. The low wages received, gave the laborers little chance of ever earning enough money to be able to acquire land of their own and become independent agriculturalists. To attain any success they needed to learn the English language, receive better pay, and be given good land for gardens, and to raise sugar cane to get additional revenue to supplement their meagre wages. It was imperative, therefore, that the authorities in Washington be fully informed, and they took action to do so.

The Pahao Hawaii Group Lists Complaints

The group employed on the Pahoa plantation in Hawaii met at a meeting on Dec. 1, 1910 and made a list of grievances. Reading the list it becomes apparent that low wages were not the sole cause of dissatisfaction. When the Pahoa meeting was called most members had been working there for eleven months. It seems that they could not tolerate conditions and treatment received any longer, and since they lacked the knowledge of English, they wrote their complaints in Russian. These were submitted to the authorities by Mrs. Warwarrow. The first complaint was that the laborers were not treated in a humane manner by the lunas and the bosses. The lunas maltreated the men and wrested cane knives out of their hands. (This, no doubt, would have the man without anything to protect himself against physical abuse.)

In some cases, as in the case of Wozelowsky and Chobotariw, all the wages were taken to cover cost of produce taken at the store, leaving the families penniless.

Perepelkin who worked as a carpenter was promised $1.00 a day, but was paid only 85¢ a day.

When the men protested about unfair treatment and one man was able to act as interpreter, he was subjected to verbal abuse, being called "a fool, an agitator, a devil and god. . .(an English slang word)".

The laborers then left the plantation and started for Hilo but the boss would not let them camp overnight on the road and drove them away.

Complaint of Olaa Plantation

Mr. Novotarov and other men who worked on the Olaa plantation on the 17th mile claimed that the store kept $17.45 from Mr. Salinko's wages; $10.00 from Medividiev; and $4.00 from Harasym Pipko in spite of the fact that none of the men took any provisions or goods at the store.

Other grievances were about charging for goods: flour cost $1.85. Available in other stores for $1.65; potatoes $3.00 for 100 lbs., available at $2.50. This much may be said to the credit of the boss: when called by the laborers, he made the plantation storekeeper make full restitution.

The men asked the boss for an increase in wages or they would go to another plantation. He told them no other plantation would hire them. They left anyway.

It appears ludicrous why the planters would not raise the wages to $1.00 a day, what the laborers requested, for they were considered to be good workers.

Harasym Pipko's Explanation[1]

According to his petition the first group of laborers left Harbin on the 14th of September, 1909, and on arrival were sent to work on plantations in the Hilo area; but due to unfavorable conditions and inadequate salary, they, like the laborers on other plantations in the other islands, went on strike.

The following is Harasym's Petition translated into English:

Explanation

At the time of publication of the recruiting for America in Harbin many in-habitants of Harbin wrote to America for Mr. Perelstrous and Mr. Atkinson to come. When people learned of the arrival of the agents for the purpose of recruiting for America, all the inhabitants of Harbin, men who were working as well as men without work came together. Mr. Perelstrous when asked about the wages in America assured that the wages are very good and that everythig is as cheap as in Harbin, products as well as clothing. The salary of a man is 45 rubles and women and girls 20 to 22 rubles a month; a boy of 14 years can receive 22 and 38 rubles a month. About dollars we did not know anything.

Owing to Mr. Perelstrous's statement everybody agreed to go to America and they began to sell their properties nearly for nothing; what had been sold was nearly given away. When everything was sold we reported to Mr. Perelstrous that we were ready to go and he told us that we would leave on September 14th. Mr. Perelstrous told us further that when we arrive in America we would receive free of charge, house, firewood and light, having lived three years in the house, same had to be our own with one acre of land. Should we like to leave the house after three years we would receive instead $300.00, which is in Russian money 600 rubles. Everybody was very glad and agreed to go at September 14th, when we left Harbin.

October 10, 1909 we arrived at the Hawaiian Islands and went to the planta-tion, we received houses and firewood but no light and there we found out immediately we had been deceived. Besides that we learned from Mr. Perelstrous as we entered the train that our salary would be paid from that very same day we entered the train. We were told that here in America does not exist such a rule to pay a man who does not work and we knew that we had been deceived.

---

[1] Harasym Pipko's Explanation, National Archives, Washington, D.C.

Three days later we went to work and when we had been working one month we were told to have a salary of 22 dollars a month. We could not work enough to receive $22.00, we earned $20.00, some $18.00 and $17.00 and $15.00. They began to take money for the store and we did not have anything left of the wages we earned. We had yet to pay out of our own pocket; who had money could pay, who did not have any was indebted as high as $43.00 and $22.00 and to $20.00. Therefore, it has been very hard for us, how much ever we earned everything was kept by the plantation. We decided to ask for a raise and did so, and we told them that according to the agreement with Mr. Perelstrous who recruited us we had to receive 45.00 rubles as a monthly salary and that the house would be our own after 3 years, should somebody prefer to leave the house after three years he had to receive $300.00 instead. The manager laughed at us and told us that we had been deceived. We then asked him to give us $1.00 a day but he answered that he could not do so. We decided to leave the plantation and went to the saw-mill in Pahoa, Puna, where they paid everybody $1.00 a day. Our situation is very bad but we cannot go anywhere else. There are parties who do not own a single dollar so that we have to wait on them sometime. There are families of 7 to 8 members and only one of them is working, these poor families never will see their native land again and it is impossible for these families to go to the continent.

Strikers Meeting Called for the 6th of December, 1910

The meeting called for the 6th of December did take place with some 150 striking laborers in attendance. Those assembled also listed their grievances and elected a committee that drew up a petition which was presented to Danl. J. Keefe, Commissioner-General.

In their petition written in Russian the striking laborers listed their grievances:

> When the first party. . .arrived in Honolulu, and divided into groups and were taken to different plantations there has been disappointment for all of them. The houses had been given to them, but decidedly they did not get anything at all, no stove, nothing that had been promised but (at) the plantation stores (they) pointed out to them, and they were told: "here you may buy whatever you want:" Everybody found out that he had been cheated and they had to thank all this to the fact that they could not understand the English (sic) language.

Some of the laborers who acquired cookstoves did not get them free, for each month one dollar was deducted to pay for them. They were not only deceived, but exploited. Their houses did not measure up to those advertised. Some were without roofs or floors.

> We worked until the first pay day and went to the office to receive money, (but) we received a piece (of) paper according to which we were in debt at the plantation store on account of dearness of the products and for the charge for tools as follows: for a cane knife 75¢, a laborer number 50¢, file 15¢, a little box for the thicket 5¢ a.s.f. (and so follows) on

At the end of the month some were still in debt at the company store, where the prices for goods purchased were high, and there was little variety and items such as meat not listed — being unavailable.

Besides the work day was made longer due to the long distances the men had to walk from camp to the fields. It was, therefore, not a ten hour day, as promised and they complained further:

> Instead of having a 10-hour day, we were at the disposition of the lunas and bosses for 12 to 14 hours. . .what we found out about the 12 to 14-hour day we could not stand (it) and we did not believe and could not believe that in the country of freedom such a treatment of laborers was possible.

The laborers call the officials, and the planters' "leeches" — sucking out the last drop of blood from the workers. Consequently, a committee was formed which tried to appeal to the enlightened American Society. They concluded their grievances of the laborers with the following paragraph:

> It seems enough and these facts are given that everybody may be shocked, but there are still facts more shameful for America, characteristic for the moral side of a civilized country. These facts lay in the intercourse with laborers. Such treatment as a foul (unclear) and not seldom the lunas treat unfortunate Russian women with blows in the teeth. Unpardonable! All around deception and disgraceful treatment caused us to leave the plantations.

The members elected by strikers at the Honolulu meeting signed the petition. They were: Jurko Wasyliw, M. Tsybish, W. Okunev, Balayn and T. Karpshak.

Anisim Vishneski who was interviewed at Wailea on the Big Island provided the following information:

> He said he was 44 years old, married with a wife and five children, the oldest girl was 16 and the only boy 14 years old. He worked as a mill hand and earned $1.00 a day, but at the end of the month, he not only did not have any money left but was in debt at the plantation store. As a railway conductor in Manchuria he earned 50 rubles a month but it went further as everything was cheaper; therefore, his condition was worse in Hawaii. The following were the prices he paid at the store.

Flour	$1.50 to $1.70 a bag
Potatoes	2¼ cents per pound
Sugar	5 cents per pound
Rice	6 cents per pound
Shoes	$2.00 a pair
Soap	10 cents per cake

All quotations and the petition are as found — translated from Russian — National Archives, Washington, D.C.

Some of these were more and some were less than in the city stores. Vishneski stated that:

> I didn't find anything as they told me. They said that we would get a house and land and water. We have no water and no land and no house. There are two families in my house and I have two rooms, only, for my family.

> Perelstrous and Atkinson told us that each family would get six acres of land but they did not give the families any land.

Mr. Vishneski's testimony seems to suggest that all kinds of promises were made, but none kept. It is difficult to understand why Mr. Vishneski had to share his home with another family.

Testimony of Plantation Manager

Credit must be given to the Inspector-in-Charge of the investigation for having the witnesses testify under oath and for having the plantation manager interrogated. (There is no evidence that he also testified under oath.)

Mr. Wilson, Plantation Manager stated as follows:

Q: **Mr. Wilson, you are, I believe, the Manager of this plantation?**
A: Yes.

Q: **How many . . . have you working here?**
A: 26 at the end of last month.

Q: **Have you had more than 26?**
A: Yes, we have lost 10 since pay day.

Q: **Have you land to offer them?**
A: They can have land the same as other nationalities if they want it.

Information, however is not available to show whether the land "made available" was suitable for the growing of a garden.

Q: **Then you are prepared to give them land if they want it?**
A: Yes.

Q: **Do you consider "them" good laborers?**
A: Yes, but they won't stay, they wander about.

Q: **Are they adapted to the work of the plantation?**
A: Yes.

It is interesting to receive Mr. Wilson's testimony that the immigrants from Harbin were good workers. However, it appears that they were disenchanted and not interested in staying in Hawaii; they wanted to go to the Mainland.

Chapter 19

Importation of Ukrainian Contract Workers
From Manchuria Ends In Failure

After the regrettable incident at the Honolulu police station where the pro-testing laborers from Camp Ilawaii were clubbed and dispersed, further marching protests ceased and the unemployed laborers accepted work wherever they could. However, with the arrival of the contract laborers on the boat "Korea" on March 7, 1910, the recruiting of laborers from Man-churia came to an abrupt halt. Nevertheless, the "Korea" group, like the first group, seemed to accept employment and created no disturbances or made protests about misrepresentations. It may be that this group was recruited by Perelstrous and Atkinson in the rural villages similar to Alexiev, from where the first group came and seemed to have been made up solely of people from the Ukraine. It appears that these people were prepared to endure hardships until such time as they would be able to establish themselves otherwise.

For the record, the laborers from Manchuria were transported to Hawaii in the following boats: "Siberia" which brought two separate groups; "S.S. Mongolia" also brought a large group — and the others came on "Teno Maru" and the "Korea".

From the information published by the Board of Immigration the number to come from Manchuria to Hawaii "amounted to 1,799 at a total cost of $139,021.59 (exclusive of the quarantine costs of $17,735.79 incurred in Honolulu. "Of the number introduced," the report states, "only a little more than 60 per cent accepted plantation employment."[1]

The Manchurian project ended with the termination of recruitment in Man-churia. It actually was a failure, and the losses were suffered not only by the Board of Immigration, but also by the planters and contract laborers. The decision of the Board to interrupt further recruitment appears justified in view of the troubles that occurred; and further recruitment would have been difficult, no doubt, as by this time the interested recruits in Manchuria must have been dissuaded after receiving letters from Hawaii, informing them about the unfavorable conditions of work, and a warning to be wary about signing contracts. In addition to this, the Russian authorities made good capital of the problems that arose, and had "The Journal of Commerce and Industry" publish a warning advising people not to emigrate to Hawaii.[2]

Planters' Dilemma

Although 60 percent of the laborers who accepted employment on plan-tations were rated as very good workers, their numbers were not large

---

[1] Appendix of 1909-1913, Board of Immigration Report, p. 4.
[2] McLaren, p. 48.

enough to satisfy the expanding needs of the sugar cane industry. The planters, therefore, were in a quandry; as depending on a large influx from Harbin, they suspended further recruitment of Portuguese laborers from the Azores, and that source seemed to be difficult to tap again. The Hawaiian "haoles" were disappointed, too, as this — at least for the time being — shattered their hopes of attracting large numbers of European settlers. Consequently, the planters had to request the Board of Immigration to look elsewhere for a fresh supply of labor. However, neither the Board nor the planters seemed to profit from their past experiences. They failed to make changes and, to raise wages: Had a fair wage been established for work on plantations, and in spite of problems that occurred — the laborers from Manchuria would have flocked to the Islands. Large number of contract workers left for the Mainland, and the planters showed concern over losing good laborers, some of them, therefore, advanced suggestions that Perelstrous be sent to San Francisco to induce them to return. The suggestion, however, was not put into practice.

In making further appraisal of the factors that contributed to the failure, it must be stated that the two agents selected to carry out recruitment of labor in Manchuria, Perelstrous and Atkinson, were also at fault. They were not adequately selective in signing up contract laborers. It was the laborers of the second group that led to the troubles which evolved. It is regrettable that in most of the countries where European people could settle as immigrants there often were unscrupulous agents to exploit the situation — to bilk and misguide the people and create confusion. It is difficult to assess to what degree the agents connected with the importation of the labor to Hawaii practised deception. However, it is definite that there was inadequate information provided to the immigrants, with respect to comparative value of the money — the ruble to the dollar.

Besides Perelstrous and Atkinson, there were other Russian-speaking agents who participated. The first was *Captain P.A. Demens* who helped in inducing the Molokans to go to Hawaii. And who was he? (Invariably these agents in coming to the U.S.A. would adopt an English name.) Captain Demens was no other than *P.A. Tvorsky* who claimed that he was a liberal nobleman and an owner of a fortune, who evidently, escaped with his life from Russia, and did well in the New Country. How he attained his captaincy is unknown.

Captain Demens encouraged the Molokans to resettle in Kauai, and when they did, the "Los Angeles Times" reported that the, "Molokans were virtual slaves under a long-term contract, and were paid seventy-five cents for a ten-hour day working in the 'sugar swamps'."[3]

Then there was Captain Samuel Johnson, another agent, who acted as interpreter in dealing with the Molokans. He was born *Samuel Ignatieff* in the Don region, educated in Cossack schools and later received naval training. In Hawaii he was a member of the National Guard, but was not available as interpreter when trouble arose with the Harbin group.

The agent J. Atkinson was born in the "Far East" and, appears was of non-Russian extraction. His father was Alatou Tumchiboulac (Atkinson).

---

[3] Ibid., p. 35.

Whether Perelstrous changed his name — as others did — is difficult to ascertain. He, however, appears to have been a man of above average education and stated that he had been a contractor on the Trans-Siberian Railroad. His pamphlet about Hawaii distributed among the people in Manchuria was well-prepared, but did not provide accurate information.

One significant thing about the agents was that they were available when each new project started, but were no place to be found when troubles arose. That was the case with Perelstrous and Atkinson during the Honolulu march of the laborers.

Ukrainian and Other Laborers Big Losers

In all this Hawaiian turmoil with laborers from Manchuria, the Ukrainian people that were anxious to get out of Manchuria were the big losers. According to authorative historians* the Ukrainian group constituted 60 per cent of the Europeans induced to settle on the available lands in Manchuria. They, too, were the group that was eager to resettle in other lands to free themselves from the Russian juggernaut. The failure of the Hawaiian plantation project, however, denied thousands of them an opportunity to emigrate to the Mainland of the U.S.A.

As the immigration of Ukrainians and other ethnic groups from Harbin ended, and many of the group left for the Mainland, San Francisco and Los Angeles, those who were unable or unprepared to leave, seemed to gravitate to Honolulu. However, there is no evidence that they attempted to organize any cultural or religious centres. This is verified by the Archbishop of the Holy Trinity Church in Honolulu. This Anglican Archbishop realized in 1916 that there was a need for a clergyman to minister to a sizeable number of residents of the Orthodox faith living in the city, and stated that his clergy, "had ministered to these people when called upon for baptisms, marriages, and burials, but that the people needed someone who could speak their language and lead them in worship to which they had been accustomed."[4] One may assume with a reasonable degree of certainty that 95 per cent of the immigrants from the Manchurian country were members of the Greek Orthodox faith.

The efforts made by the Archbishop met with success: on contacting the Orthodox Archbishop of New York, a clergyman was sent to Hawaii. Reverend John T. Dorosh and his wife arrived in Honolulu on December 29, 1916, on January 6*, 1917 "with a procession when people (some 200 in number) carried lighted candles around the outside of the Cathedral."[5]

This first Orthodox Christmas service conducted in Honolulu, no doubt, made the displaced Ukrainians and Russians realize more keenly their isola-

---

* V. Kubijovych. *Encyclopedia of Ukraine* Vol. 1, University Press, Toronto, Passim pp. 857-860.

[4] *"Hawaii, 1778 - 1920 from the Viewpoint of a Bishop"*, Paradise of the Pacific, Honolulu, 1924., p. 342.

* The Orthodox Church celebrated Christmas according to the Julian calendar. Participating, evidently, in the first Orthodox Church service were, also, Japanese residents of the Orthodox faith.

[5] Ibid.

tion. Their inability to acquire land and any hope that more of their people would, in due time, arrive in Honolulu made them come to the conclusion that they had to make another change — and so did Rev. Dorosh. After a year of missionary work among his people and ministry to the Japanese laborers of the Orthodox faith, he returned to the Mainland.

The reason for the leaving of Rev. Dorosh was a matter of having to accept the situation that ensued: "nearly all of his congregation left Honolulu, some for the coast and some for Siberia. . ."[6] where they were promised land if they returned. . .

The departure of Rev. John Dorosh and his congregation from Hawaii virtually ended the last chapter of the *Hawaiian Ordeal* for the Ukrainian contract workers in the "Paradise Islands."

Rev. Dr. J.C.E. Riotte, 1986, with an old Russian Censer.*

---

[6] Ibid., p. 343.
* See Appendix I.

PART III

Tracing
Descendants
of
Contract
Workers

Sunday visit: sugar cane workers from Western Ukraine.

Chapter 20

Tracing Descendants of Contract Workers from Ukraine

Tracing the descendants of any group of people who have gone from their native land to a far-flung country is not a simple matter; tracing the descendants of the Ukrainian immigrants who first came to Hawaii in 1897, was found to be difficult. It was difficult more so as the immigration to the Islands ceased very abruptly nearly eighty years ago. However, the question most often asked by the people who got interested in the research project dealing with sugar cane workers, from the Ukraine was: "How many of their descendants still live in Hawaii? Therefore, to be able to answer this question and to make the research-commenced eleven years ago — more comprehensive and complete, another trip was made to the Islands.

The investigation was started on the Island of Oahu to determine if any people from the Ukraine still live in the largest centre in the Islands — Honolulu. It was possible to contact two only but they are newcomers. One was Dr. Ihor Kudelski who moved to Honolulu from Chicago, and the other was Rev. J. Riotte, a Catholic clergyman of the Byzantian Rite trained in the Ukrainian Catholic seminary in Canada. But it was impossible to trace any descendants of the original groups. Enquiries at the Hamilton Library, University of Hawaii and in the State Archives of Hawaii did not bring immediate results, until a school teacher who taught in the Big Island provided valuable leads. She informed us that there were some descendants in the Mountain View area, and the Verbiske family is well known. In addition to this she told us that there is a road named after one of the early settlers.

The Hilo librarians were most helpful and provided us with the name of Mr. Bill Yeomans. Since it was not possible to contact Mr. Yeomans by phone, the teachers at the Mountain View school and the women at the Post Office directed us to the home of Mr. Michael Lizak who still lives in his family home with his brother Louis. Mr. Lizak directed us further up the highway and we found the Pszyk Road and followed it through the sugar cane fields to the farm where Mr. Yeomans, and the two Pszyk sisters live on their parents' 50-acre farm.

Michael Lizak Recalls Events Connected with the Settlement

Mr. Lizak was most willing and helpful in providing information about his parents and the other settlers who came to Hawaii on the "Glade" and were some of a small number that decided eventually to settle on land and then remained in the Big Island.

*   *   *   *   *

149

Sign Showing The Pszyk Road

Michael Lizak: It is regrettable that you did not come sooner: You are four months late. Had my mother lived a little longer she would have been a hundred years old. It is sad that she passed away four months ago. She came to the Island as a young girl. She was Anna Werbiski and maybe the oldest settler of the contract workers of 1898. Her mind was excellent, but I guess the dampness and the cold in the Olaa Rain Forest region homestead were hard on her feet and she finally had to go to a personal care home where she died.

She was a Verbiske (Werbiski) and came to Honolulu with her parents in 1898 on the vessel "Glade." From there they were sent to the Big Island where grand-

Mr. L. Lizak, holding John, Mrs. Annie Lizak and Mr. Andruch Werbiski and young Frank standing.

father, Andruch Werbiski, worked as a contract worker in the Onomea plantation. Mother told us that the native Hawaiian were very good to the European
contract workers and used to bring them vegetables and fruit. This helped the
people during the first few months on the plantation.

As mother grew older and the friends she knew passed away, she complained
at times that she had no one to reminisce with about the early days and about
her native country. She told us that in the Old Country she had to herd sheep.
She did not like that work. Here she said that though the first few years were
miserable, but when the contracts were cancelled, though the people worked
hard, they were free.

Anna and Michael Pszyk, Mountain View H1 (circa 1903).

My parents were young when they got married and they went with the other settlers up the volcano way to settle on the homestead. When the settlers found life on the homesteads most unsatisfactory and began to leave, my parents, I think, were among the last ones to leave the homestead and come to Mountain View.

Life was hard on the homesteads, and for the women left alone with the children while the men went to work on plantations or on the railroad, it was as hard as the olia trees they were trying to clear. It rained often and it was hard to have much of a garden, but in time they managed to have a good garden, had chickens and pigs and some even had cows. Once the railroad was completed to the Olaa plantation from Mountain View it was easier for the men to come home during the weekends.

I remember my mother telling me that she was alone when the first baby came. She was in labor when she heard some voices along the trail and she called. Two young girls came in. They were bright girls and followed Mother's instructions and the baby was delivered. After that mother always spoke of these girls with affection and praise, saying: "Wherever they may be at this time, I hope that the Good Lord is good to them." It may be that they were the motherless girls who lived alone on the homestead during the week while their father was away at work. As if that wasn't enough, my mother was caught unprepared for the delivery of another baby, and I think it was I who came into the world this time. But by then she was more mature and more experienced and could take care of herself all alone.

Life on the homestead, as I remember it, was as grey as the weather. Our small home was surrounded by vegetation and there was little beauty to admire. In time, however, the women of the settlement with the help of the children pushed back the forest and planted roses around their homes. The roses grew in profusion and now anytime I go to visit my uncle John Verbiske in Volcano the roses in the Verbiske yard remind me of the roses on our homestead.

Before there was a school and I understand it was a long time before the authorities built the school they promised there wasn't much for the children to do; after they completed their assigned chores, they were free. Even in my day this freedom was short-lived: we had to guard our chicken flock. You see as the boats came to Hilo, the rats got out of the vessels and swam ashore. Soon they became a pest. Somebody had a bright idea that if the mongooses were brought to the Big Island, they would in time exterminate the rats. The little squirrel-like mongoose who could finish a snake in quick order did not seem to have any inclination to tackle the rat, and the two lived in peace. As a consequence, both the rats and the mongoose multiplied. The mongoose, though, seemed to have a liking for chicken and would raid the coops and our chicken flock began to decrease in number. We boys, therefore, were pressed into service to keep the mongooses in control.

The Mongoose War

The pesky little creatures were hard to scare away, and hard to trap as we did not have a proper kind of trap. When we set the ordinary trap, the chickens got into them first. Finally the men on the homestead designed a box-like trap, like those they had in the Old Country, and father made us one. We would set this contraption and place a dead chicken as bait. Sooner than we expected the mongoose would spring the trap. We then would place one end of the trap into a sack and shake him out by opening the end slightly. Once this was done we would let the dog finish the job.

We Moved to Mountain View

My father worked on a plantation close to Mountain View and finally became a luna. He received better pay and a house was made available for us. Life became easier for my Mother, and we children had a better opportunity to go to school. The houses on the plantations were clustered close together. They were barely five feet away from the neighbors house; one had to learn quickly how to live with the neighbors. In time the house became ours and as it was small, from time to time, my father would add to it. We have modern facilities and have lived in it ever since. My Mother had to learn English and we children learned English, and Portugese and Hawaiian and some Japanese. We all adjusted to life in the Mountain View area and my parents enjoyed their own people who had moved here too.

I went to school and then went to work, soon I became a carpenter. Though all of us had our start working on the cane field. I have lived in this area all my life. The first time I left was to see my father in the hospital in Honolulu. He took a stroke and died there. I went to Oahu, leaving the Big Island for the second time to bring my Father's body here for burial.

My three brothers left the Islands and went to the Mainland. They worked there for years, and when my brother died there of cancer I went to the funeral and that was the first time I went to the Mainland. Louis worked in Los Angeles for over thirty years and the last time I was there was when I went to bring him back home. With Mother's care he has regained his health exceptionally well.

Things kept improving for us here and we had a good life. My parents adjusted well to Hawaii and enjoyed it and in time learned to like poi. I like poi and still use poi on my bread instead of butter. For a long time my Mother used to cook Old Country dishes and we liked them. During Christmas and Easter there were always special dishes and fine baking. And we had many visits from our friends.

Louis Lizak: There was something I did not understand, and still don't understand. Why was there always a bowl of sweetened boiled wheat to start the Christmas Eve dinner, and why Christmas was celebrated by some people two weeks later than the regular Christmas.)

The young people, tried to acquire a trade or a profession, though most of the boys tried their hand at cane cutting. We had one teacher, one

Michael and Louis Lizak beside their Mountain View home.

postmistress, (the Durbanuik girl was one for years), and the Hoculak boy became a clergyman. There are some on other islands — two Pszyk boys, Frank and Bill are on the Island of Maui. The rest moved to the Mainland.

My parents told us that when Dr. Russel was still living on his plantation on the Volcano Road, people went to see him when they needed medical assistance. He did not attempt to cure anything serious, but would prescribe pills for minor ailments or dress a wound of less serious nature.

There are very few descendants of the original settlers left here, but we who are left keep in touch and get along exceptionally well.

The Zembiks

I am certain that the descendants of Holowatys, Romans, Durbanuiks and others may have an interesting story to tell you about the coming of their people to Hawaii and life on the Big Island if only one could contact some of them.

At this time I* would like to add something abut the Zembik family. As far as I know they did not come to Hawaii with the first two groups that came on the Glade. Where they came from I do not know, but theirs is an interesting story, particularly how Mr. Zembik wanted to go in to dairy farming in a big way — and he worked hard at it.

---

* As related by Michael Lizak of Mountain View, Feb. 1985.

It is surprising how, if a man sets his mind to it, he can develop his project rather quickly. That was the case with Mr. Zembik. Before long he had a small herd of milch cows and the whole family worked at herding the cows, milking them and churning some of the cream into butter. Mr. Zembik took the butter to the village of Mountain View for sale. Soon he found out that his project was in trouble.

He tried to sell his butter to the Portuguese people, but they did not seem to use butter; their women cooked with oil. And as far as the Hawaiians were concerned they did not buy butter because they used poi. As a result, after each trip to town, he had to bring some of his butter home. Then he had a serious problem: he had no refrigeration on the farm, and the coolest place he could find to keep the surplus butter was to cover it and place it under the bed. However, in the warm climate the butter would not keep long and by the time he was making another trip to town it would turn rancid and had to be thrown out. There was no profit in doing this but he persisted with his enterprise and had the whole family working hard and getting nowhere. Finally he accepted his wife's suggestion and discontinued the production of a large amount of butter.

Zembiks Meet in Hawaii

In 1900* four families from the village of Zbaraz in the Western Ukraine emigrated to settle in Canada. When they reached the port city where they were to board a vessel for the ocean crossing, the agents talked one of the Zembik brothers to change his mind and instead of going to Canada to go to Brazil; transportation for the whole family was free.

The other Zembik brother, Felix, his wife Louisa and children, and Stotskis and the Chepys and their children came to Manitoba, Canada and first settled on smaller acreages north of Beausejour in the Brokenhead district. But when they found out that homesteads were available in the Interlake area, they resettled north of Winnipeg and named their new district Zbaraz. In time the two Zembik brothers established communications and corresponded for many years.

I grew up in the Zbaraz district and as a young girl lived with my grandparents most of the time. My Grandmother seemed to like to tell me stories about the Old Country and their coming to Canada. I listened to the letters read by my grandfather. Those he received from his brother in Brazil were most pathetic. He informed us that Brazil was a hot and humid country, and that they settled in some kind of a swamp where it was next to impossible to develop any land for cultivation. He stated that the future was not too bright for his children and that there was nowhere to earn any money so he could bring his family to Canada. This I remember well for it was often repeated by my grandparents: "Brother," he wrote, "if there was dry land from here to your country, we would be prepared to walk all the way to

---

* As related by Mrs. Mary Luty who grew up in Zbaraz, Manitoba. (Nov. 1985).
(Additional information provided by Mrs. Mary Stonga and Mrs. Bill Uruski from the old Zbaraz district.)

reach your Canada. For from what you wrote me, though you work hard, you live in Paradise."

My grandfather died in 1920, and as there wasn't anyone to write letters using the Latin alphabet, correspondence ceased and we heard no more from Brazil.

A couple of years ago, my uncle and aunt, the Stongas, and another couple from Zbaraz made a trip to Hawaii and looking over the names in the phone book found that there was a Zembik listed. It seems to me, and I may just remember this vaguely; that we did know in Zbaraz that some people in Brazil were recruited to go to Hawaii to work on sugar cane plantation; and that one of Zembik's sons joined a group and took his family out of Brazil being unable to make a living in that hot country. Consequently, Mrs. Stonoga phoned this Zembik family. They were staying in a hotel and he agreed to come to the hotel to see them. Mrs. Stonoga says: "We were sitting in the hotel lobby and when I saw a man walk in I was sure he was a Zembik for he looked like uncle Walter."

* * * * *

Interview with Helen Richardson-Pszyk

It was possible for us to find the Pszyk road according to the directions given by Mr. Michael Lizak and we arrived at a Hawaiian farm. There are two homes on the farm: one that of the Bill Yeomans family and the other the pioneer home of the Pszyk family where the two daughters Helen and Agnes, seem to live comfortably. We interviewed Mrs. Helen Richardson who brought us up to date on her family and life of the immigrants on a Hawaii farm.

My parents Michael Pszyk and my mother, Anna Markewicz, came to Hawaii as young people and were married early in their teens. Father was employed on the plantation and they seemed to live close to my grandparents. My grandfather, Peter Markewicz, was employed as a blacksmith most of the time and earned little better wages than the average.

When the settlers were acquiring homesteads, my parents bought a fifty-acre farm beside that of my Grandfather and in addition to work on the plantation he began to clear some land and go into developing a small herd of cows. My father earned a little money from the sale of wood. They started to keep cows and sold milk, cream and butter in the village. The pasturage was good and in this warm country there was no need to provide forage for the winter. Father built a house of the type built on the plantations for the workers. It had to be raised off the ground for better ventilation. We are still living in it.

As I was told by my parents and as I remember, on the start we were rather isolated — we virtually lived in the bush. To start with my father blazed a path so that they were able to walk out to the Volcano road. He then widened it into a trail, but it wasn't very satisfactory to haul wood to the village for which there was good demand, and take milk and other products. There

Mrs. Helen Richardson

Mrs. Helen Richardson standing beside an outdoor oven on her parents farm.

Peter Markewicz, the Mountain View blacksmith, and local residents, June 1913. (H. Richardson Coll.)

was a limit what one could haul in a cart.

Finally my father approached the council to have them make the trail into a road, but there was little interest in such a project. He, eventually, widened the trail himself and made it into a passable road. Then the council took it over and named it the Pszyk Road, and rightly so. . .

Ours became a large family. There were thirteen in all. My mother was a busy woman and we had to help her. To help with the cooking an outdoor oven was built. Grandfather made the grate and the doors for it and it was built like a beehive, rounded on top and hard-finished with cement. My grandfather said that it was no use building a clay outdoor oven like those they built in the Old Country as the constant rains would wash the clay away.

The heavy rains provided a problem. When it did rain a lot and the sun did not come out to dry out things, the interior of the house would get very damp and then finally mould would start to appear on the walls.

In the early days we adhered to the old traditions when celebrating Easter and Christmas; mother prepared special foods and at Christmas there was always a Christmas tree. Mother saw to it that each child got a Christmas present. At Easter, colored eggs were a must. It was hard to get the ingredients for the coloring of eggs, so mother used the Old Country approach: eggs were boiled with dry onion skins and they came out beautifully orange, and some times yellow.

I also seem to recall that when visitors came to visit on Christmas Eve, they would throw wheat on the floor and under the table as they greeted the family.

Children first attended the Glenwood school which was organized for the children of the homesteaders, but as the settlers moved away the school

(L-R) Julia Pszyk, grandson Yeomans, Helen P. Richardson and Bill Yeomans. (M.E. Coll. Mnt. View, HI. Feb., 1985).

population changed and, my sister Alice was likely the only one of the children from the Olaa forest children left. (Miss Lopaz was also a teacher in the school close to the Pszyks).

All we children did considerable work helping with the care of the cattle and milking of cows and then churning the cream into butter.

I got married when I was very young. Bill Yeomans is my son. I have a nice grandson, too. They look after us very well; they live in the next house on this farm. We are not doing much with the farm now and when we are gone, we will leave it the way it was in my parents' time. However, we shall put together some things my grandfather made and maybe as you suggest, turn them over to the museum in Hilo. My son Bill serves as a fire ranger and he knows the old homestead area well.

(Mr. Bill Yeomans: The old homestead area is not easy to reach. The best way to get there is by jeep and I shall be glad to take you there on Sunday. However, it is a fairly rough terrain and not a good place to travel on a very wet day. My son says that when he finishes high school he will take training to become a forest ranger too, but one cannot get training here and he may have to go to the Mainland to complete his training in Oklahoma.)

For years I used to run the school cafeteria and enjoyed it. Now that I am retired, I enjoy life on this parental farm.

(Julia: Helen always liked school and she was good at it, but I did not like studying — I would much rather herd cows and look after the farm work. I really didn't want to go to school).

In the early days, people used to get together during Sundays and holidays. That was the time that the older ones used to talk about the Old Country. On the start the language of conversation was either Polish or Ukrainian depending on the visitors. We children soon began to converse in English only. There were the Pszyks and the Zembiks and Gombskis and the Lizaks and the Werbiskis (Verbiskes) Durbeniuks and others who made up the membership of the small community. Church services were held in the old

Children of Glenwood school, Miss Orvis, teacher. Alice Pszyk (front centre) the only descendant of pioneer settlers. c. 1912.

Sophie Pszyk and the favorite calf. (Note the type of fence in use).

Catholic church served by a Portuguese-speaking clergyman. Then we had a visit from Rev. Tom Hoculak, after he finished his training, but we had no other organization of our own. In time the young people began to inter-marry with others and many moved away. The older people, of course, began to die and the community started to decrease. Now there are only a few of us left.

I have a picture taken at the funeral of one of the senior members of our community. In the twenties the group was still fairly large.

Rev. Tom Hoculak*

Of those who came to Hawaii on H.F. Glade as children·was one Demko Hoculak. He was five years old in 1891 when he arrived in Hawaii with his parents. Eventually he became a priest — likely the first one of the group that came from Western Ukraine. We have the following information about him from Mr. Michael Lizak:[1]

> All I know about Rev. Tom Hoculak is that he went to Mountain View School, although I do not know to what grade. Then his family moved to California, but I have not any information about his life there until he became priest and returned to Honolulu and then to Hawaii (Big Island).
> If you want to know more about him, his brother John[2] lives in California . . .
> The priest is very old now and lives in Honolulu. He is 94 years now.

Mrs. Helen Richardson adds as follows:

> Rev. Tom Hoculak was a Catholic priest in Kau. He lived there with his father. I don't know if he is alive yet.[3]

---

[1] LS. by Michael Lizak of Mountain View, Hi to Michael Ewanchuk, December, 1985.
[2] Did not get a reply from John Hoculak.
[3] Helen Richardson of Mountain View to M. Ewanchuk.
* Spelling of name as originally recorded on the passenger list.

Funeral of Mrs. Nicholas Holowaty (circa 1922) (The picture was taken beside the old Catholic church we attended.

Standing (back row, L-R): Joe Zembik, Rev. Tom Hoculak, Michael Pszyk, Nicholas Holowaty, n.n. and n.n., John Holowaty, Peter Pszyk, Michael Holowaty, Peter Holowaty, George Holowaty, Mary Holowaty, Sophie Holowaty, Gombsky, also John Verbeske, Catherine Durbenuik (just back of the car), also toward the end of the row, Katherine Lizak, Helen Pszyk (Mrs. Richardson), Alice Pszyk, and the last man, John Roman.

Front Row: the Gombsky children: Constantine, Demetri, Victor, Zeena, and Sophie held in the arms of Mr. Gombsky. The man standing in front is Lawrence Lizak, and to the right of him, is John Verbiske. Some of those in the middle of the front row are not identified by Mrs. Richardson.

According to Michael Lizak, most of the early settlers who died were buried either in Hilo — the Curtis Town Cemetery or the Mountain View Cemetery.

Mr. Isidore Goresky when contacted in Edmonton writes:

> I checked my yearly notebooks I kept when I was superintendent of schools and find that I visited the St. Patrick's Monastery in Honolulu in 1968 where I met an old monk, Father Wenceslas (nee Demian Hoculak), who had been brought up and educated by the monastic people. He claimed his Mother was a Katherine Szrynyk from the village of Kossiv (in the Western Ukraine), but he did not know where Kossiv was . . . later . . . , I sent him a map of Ukraine with the information.

The Congregation of the Sacred Hearts, Kaneole, Hawaii provides us with additional data about Fr. Wenceslas. Rev. Demain Huculuk, (originally Demko Hoculak), the son of Tymko and Kateryna (nee Sztynik) was born in Kossow, Western Ukraine on November 13, 1892 and came to Hawaii with his parents on the H.F. Glade in 1897.

Rev. Wenceslas received his theological training in Europe. His temporary profession date was September 29, 1918 at Fuentabrabia, Spain and his perpetual profession date was at Masnuy St. Pierre. He was ordained in Tournai, Belgium on December 31, 1923.

In January 1925 he arrived in Hawaii-Kau and assumed clerical duties there, transferring to Honolulu in 1935. In 1953 he served at St. Patricks and then in 1953 became chaplain at the Kalihi Orphanage. On returning to St. Patricks in 1963, he served in a semi-retired capacity and since 1984 has been listed as being on vacation.

Rev. Demain Hoculak, the son of peasant parents from the Ukraine and Hawaii plantation workers, was likely the only one of the group who returned to Europe and then came to Hawaii to serve as a clergyman.

The Werbiskis (Verbiskes)

Of the Andruch and Magda Werbiski descendants there is only their son, John left, in Hawaii. He and his wife, Anna, the younger sister of Helen Richardson, live in Volcano, P.O. Their daughter, Maxine, a nurse in the

The Volcano crater a few miles south of the Verbiske home.

Mr. and Mrs. John Verbiske and Mr. Michael Lizak in the Verbiske yard in Volcano, P.O., HI, Feb. 1985.

(L-R) Muriel Ewanchuk, John Verbiske, Mrs. Verbiske and Michael Ewanchuk, Feb. 1985.

local hospital lives with them. And their daughter, Ludwina, Mrs. William C. Franklin, lives in Hilo. She works in the dietary department of the hospital.

The Verbiskes are living in a fine home in Volcano situated at an altitude of 4000 feet. Their yard is a bower of roses and other "exotic" flowering bushes. If Andruch Werbiski were alive, he would certainly observe that his son lives in the "Garden of Eden". It gets cool here", said Mrs. Verbiski, "we use our fireplace to keep the house comfortable in the evening. We burn olia tree wood and it is hard wood that produces heat equal to that of coal. We buy mill ends at the saw mill and find them most satisfactory.

The Volcano P.O. area is not far from the Olaa Forest Reserve where the contract workers acquired homesteads, and the colony of Russians — first brought in by Dr. Russel — was in the vicinity.

In addition to Michael and Louis Lizak, sons of Werbicki's daughter Anna, as far as we have been able to ascertain, Mr. and Mrs. Verbiske and their four children are the only other descendants of Andruch and Magda Werbicki left. Though John remembers much of the hardships or the pioneer times, there was not the opportunity to record many details. Ludwina, Mrs. Franklin, says that she lacks information about her grandparents, and that she doesn't even know the name of the village from which they came to Hawaii, but adds:

> I know that my grandparents could speak no English. . .(and neither could many of the others of their group, no doubt.) Andruch Werbickis did live on the homestead. I guess you could say they lived like pioneers — getting firewood for their wood stoves and raising their own vegetables. They had no cars and had to walk miles and miles wherever they went. The houses they lived in were wooden structures and were built far apart.[1]

Andruch Werbiski toiled under the broiling sun and in the heavy rains of Hawaii for forty years. He came to Hilo when he was 48 years old and his "Hawaiian Ordeal" ended in 1937 when he was eighty-eight. His wife, Magda was a young woman when she arrived in Hawaii. She died in 1918 at an early age of 48. Their descendants from the home of John and Anna Verbiske number four. Grandson John and the youngest grand-daughter, Susan live in California. In Hawaii, beside the two grand-daughters Maxine, and Ludwina, are two great grandchildren, the children of the William C. Franklins.

Some Came to Canada by Way of the Pacific

It has been possible to trace settlers coming from the villages of Kossiw and Slobidka in the Western Ukraine to Winnipeg, and Elfros Saskatchewan. Whether they are joined here by those who left Hawaii is unknown. However, in addition to the Mrs Derko's family, the Kucys, there were others of the Hawaiian group who joined their countrymen in Alberta. They were the Florkows, Koncohradas,Prusses, Sztyniks, Wierzbickis and it seems the

---

[1] Mrs. William C. Franklin of Hilo, Hi. to Michael Ewanchuk December 5, 1985.

Garguses -- there may have been others. Now some of their descendants live in the area north-east of Edmonton; where they seemed to have prospered. They live in such centres as Edmonton, Lamont, Mundare, and St. Michaels. We have received this information about them from Mr. Isidore Goresky of Edmonton. He writes:

> I have obtained some information and records from Mrs. Jordan . . . On one of the lists is Fabian Wierzbicki from the village of Slobidka which I know is Dzurynska Slobitka and his destination was Kaalehu, Hawaii. This was Verla Jordan's father. On the other list we find Sztynik, Felix, Tekla and Kaszia. The last one being Verla's future mother. Apparently they all were on the H.F. Glade for six months. On arrival in Hawaii they worked on different plantations from 1898 until 1902 when they left for San Francisco. Verla's mother remembers the San Francisco earthquake. Of the other records she has is a certificate of marriage of Katerina Sztynik to Fabian Wierzbicki on May 28, 1899 in Pahola on the Big Island. By the way, the Sztyniks came from Kossiw . . . Apparently, (after they completed their contracts) the Hawaii experience was enough for their parents because they returned to the Western Ukraine, but Verla finally landed in Alberta.[1]

Audruch Werbicki whose family came from Slobidka Dzhurynska and remained in Hawaii may have been related to the Fabian Wierzbicki who also came from Slobidka. It also appears that Joseph and Rozalia Wiezbicki were Fabian's parents and they returned to Western Ukraine.

As far as the Kucy's are concerned there are several in the St. Michael's-Lamont area: Dave, A., Dennis, Mrs. H., J.F. and John P. Some of these we know for certain are the descendants of D. Kucy who came from Hawaii, and are related to Mrs. Derko.

---

[1] Isidore Goresky of Edmonton to Michael Ewanchuk, March 4, 1986.

Conclusion

With this section we bring to the end a saga, a "Hawaiian Ordeal" of the Ukrainian sugar-cane workers. It is an adventure of brave and proud people who by emigrating to the New World hoped to find greater freedom and land to sustain them. However, they had to spend several years in bondage in the Paradise of the Pacific. They were willing workers, but also resolute people who resisted abuse and oppression. And like their forebearers who fought to cast-off the serfdom imposed on them by the Hapsburg and Romanov regimes, they struggled in the New World for the abrogation of unfair contracts, and with the aid of their countrymen in the United States and the leaders of the American government finally succeeded in freeing themselves from the state of being servants to the Hackfeld masters. In their struggle for freedom and in attaining it they helped to blaze the trail to freedom for the other contract workers who slaved on the Hawaiian plantations. Becoming free was the end of their strange Hawaiian interlude.

In order to conclude this study, it is necessaryt to recapitulate briefly, to restate the fact that when the first contingent of contract workers from Western Ukraine left Bremerhaven, there was three men on board the "H.F. Glade" that we have singled out for specific mention: Andruch Werbicki, Dmytro Puchalsky and Panko Yakimishyn — all three signed contracts of indenture to work on the Herr Hackfeld's plantations in Onomea on the Big Island of Hawaii. And now for the summation of their experiences.

The first of these men, Andruch Werbicki came to the Islands when he was approaching his fifties and his wife was a relatively young woman. Once their contracts were cancelled, they had the opportunity of leaving, but for family reasons, it appears, they decided to make their permanent home in Hawaii and lived out their years in the Mountain View area.

The second one, Dmytro Puchalsky, came to the Island in the prime of life and in good physical condition having just completed his military training. He was ready for adventure and hoped for a bright future for himself in the New Land. But Hawaii proved a disappointment. Having the required finances to feel somewhat independent — when the first opportunity arose — he bought his freedom from the German planter, Hackfeld and left for San Francisco where he became a free citizen and a successful businessman.

The third, Panko Yakimishyn, seemed to venture the farthest from his Hawaiian bondage. He established himself as a homesteader in Roblin, Manitoba, Canada. Like Andruch and Magda Werbicki, Panko and Ewdocha Yakimishyn toiled on land rolling back the fringe of the Duck Mountain forest. They grew grain, raised cattle and Panko cut cord wood which he hauled to Deepdale with his yoke of oxen. They never owned a car; they walked long distances to Roblin, Deepdale and Merridale, but never left their Gleneden farm. They lived in a community of relatives and friends.

In the Gleneden district they learned very little more English than they knew when they came from Hawaii for they could get along doing business in their native tongue. They had their own Ukrainian Catholic Church and their community hall. And when they died, they were burried in the St. Michael's cemetery on the hill. The Yakimishyn markers read: Panko (1834-1919); Ewdocha (1847-1913): Rest in Peace. And that's where their Hawaiian odessey ended.

(L-R) Ewdocha and Panko Yakimishyn monuments.

APPENDICES

Appendix I

Ardan, Rev. Iwan, 1871-1940, a pioneer Ukrainian Catholic priest who came to the United States in 1895 and devoted most of his time to journalism, originally as editor of "Svoboda", 1900-07; from 1918-1921 he worked with the Ukrainian diplomatic mission as secretary in Washington. He was a man of liberal views and championed the cause of labor in the U.S.A. and the contract workers in Hawaii. Recognized as the leading journalist among the early Ukrainian editors in the U.S.A.

Dmytriw, Rev. Nestor, 1863-1925, came to U.S.A. from Western Ukraine in 1895 and first served as parish priest in Mount Carmel, Pa. He was active among the Ukrainian laborers and began the first president of a fraternal benefit organization, now the Ukrainian National Association. He was editor of "Svoboda", 1896-07. In 1897 he accepted a position as immigration agent with the Canadian government, toured Canada and was the first Ukrainian Catholic clergyman to visit the Ukrainian settlers (Sifton's Settlers) in Western Canada. In 1898 he returned to the United States. In his many articles he discouraged the Ukrainian emigrants from going to settle in Argentine or Brazil on the lands selected for them by the agents, and also about signing contracts to go to Hawaii.

Dole, Sandford B., one of the missionary scions born in the islands, who opposed the contract system "from principle, because I think it is wrong," urged unregulated immigration by free men as the best way to gain "settlers and citizens rather than convicts and coolies." Good men and families would come from all parts of the world, if Hawaii would offer them wages, homesteads, and citizenship.

Honcharenko, Rev. Ahapius, 1832-1916 is considered to be the first known educated Ukrainian to come to the United States. He was a refugee escaping Russian arrest for his liberal views while attached to the Russian embassy in Greece. He first lived in New York where he taught at the St. John's Episcopal seminary, and also, in 1865 he laid a corner stone for the first Greek Orthodox Church in New Orleans, LA.

In 1867 he moved to San Francisco where he and his wife, Albina Chitti, (whom he married in the U.S.A.) published the "Alaska Herald" and were engaged in assisting many refugees escaping from the Russian maws in Siberia. He also prepared a Russian-English grammar and a Phrase Book to help the American official deal with the former Russian citizens in Alaska.

Rev. Honcharenko was supposed to have known the great Ukrainian poet Taras Shevchenko and used to quote him periodically in his paper. In San Francisco he took strong action against the Russian officials and even the Russian bishop of the Orthodox church. He was planning to organize a move to form an independent area consisting of Manchuria and parts of Siberia. During the years he lived in fear of being captured by the Russians and returned to serve in the Siberian prison.

Eventually he moved to Hayward, California where he had a small farm he called "Ukraina." Rev. Honcharenko died in 1916 and is buried beside his wife on their farm "Ukraina". Though their graves are marked, they are now found in the cow pasture, and no action has been taken to make their resting place accessible or declared an historic site.

Kochan, Theodore, The American "Svoboda" of May 17, 1900 printed a letter received from Theodore Kochan stationed in San Pedro, Morati, Philippine Islands, who wrote: *"First because the rebellion here is nearly finished, and, second because our regiment has been in the firing line for more than a year, we have been given leave."* He must have arrived in the Philippines as a member of the American army in 1898, and must, therefore, be given credit of being the first Ukrainian to arrive in the Philippines. Theodore Kochan later came to Manitoba and was engaged as teacher and employee of the Government. Imbued with the philosophy of Leo Tolstoy he was instrumental in having the name of the post office of Oleskow changed to "Tolstoi."

Lysiansky, Captain Yuri, a Ukrainian by birth, was a captain in the Russian navy. In sailing from Europe around the Horn to reach Japan, he stopped in Hawaii where he established good relations with King Kamehameha. He, therefore, was the first Ukrainian to reach Hawaii and to circumnavigate the world. As a consequence he wrote a book, *"A Voyage Around the World in the Years 1803-4,5,&6."* He was an officer in the Russian navy having received his training in English. He knew the English language and translated his book into English. Early in the nineteenth century Captain Lysiansky also visited the United States.

The Molokans, were a break-away religious sect that came to the United States from Russia to gain religious freedom. They were organized by a Ukrainian religious activist, Ukleen, and formed a totally separate group from the Doukhobors. Ukleen returned to the Orthodox church, but the group persisted in maintaining their organization. Peter Verigon visited their colonies in the Los Angeles area trying to induce them to join his group in Canada. However, they went to Hawaii. Their experience in Hawaii was not a happy or successful one, and they returned to California.

Myshuha, Dr. Luke, a lawyer by training who came to the United States from Western Ukraine after World I as a deputy representative of the Ukrainian diplomatic mission of the Ukrainian Republic. He remained in the U.S.A. to become the editor of the "Svoboda". He was an essayist and a historian and prepared for publication a *Jubilee Book* of the Ukrainian National Association which has become a valuable reference source about the Ukrainians in the United States.

Oleskow, Prof. Joseph, a professor of agriculture who visited Canada in 1895 to investigate the opportunities for the settlement of Ukrainian farmers in Western Canada. He wrote two pamphlets in which he discouraged emigration to South America, and warned the Ukrainian farmers to be wary about the unscrupulous port agents.

Riotte, Very Rev. Dr. J.C.E., in his letter of March 27, 1986, Very Rev. J.C.E. Riotte informed us that he came to Honolulu from the Eparch of Toronto. It was Bishop Boresky's idea to establish a mission of the Ukrainian Catholic Church in Hawaii, and the Eparchy of Chicago gave the first jurisdiction to the new mission. It was Bishop Ferrario who gave his approval for the organization of "The Eastern Catholic Church Apostolate SS Cyril and Methodius of the R.C. Diocese of Honolulu, Hi. The censer I am holding came to us from the Roman Catholic Cathedral and I use it every Sunday -- 'it is Russian that much is certain' . . . I am an Episcopal Vicar for the Catholic Orientals: Ukrainians, Ruthenians, Maronites, Melkites, Armenians and even Russians."

Western Ukraine, (Halychyna) on losing its independence and falling under the Austrian hegemony was in the administrative area of Galicia. Consequently, people from that jurisdiction — Germans, Jews, Poles, Swabians and Ukrainians were all officially recorded as Galicians. In the "free world" literate and cultured Ukrainians and Poles discarded the appelation as a vestige of foreign domination. (In order not to confuse the reader, the writer calls the people by their proper ethnic name.)

Wilcox, Robert W., was a Hawaiian activist decade of the 19th century. Canadians would consider him a Hawaiian Cuthbert Grant, but Wilcox saw himself a kind of Hawaiian Garibaldi. Though he had received some engineering training in Italy, he could not receive satisfactory employment in Hawaii. He consequently despised the Hawaiian administration which was influenced by the planters. Some planters -- British, American or German and their friends were not considered gentlemen. Though Wilcox hated the white bureaucrats, he respected Dr. N.K. Russel. Wilcox was supposed to have said:

We don't want these white men who are wandering about and coming here; they are a good for nothing lot, all they want is money, and when they get it, they get up and go away. It is only the real natives of the country who have any feeling of love for their land.

White Slaves in Hawaii

After Captain Lysiansky established cordial relations with King Kamehameha, two adventurers of German extraction were sent to the Hawaiian Islands, by the Russians, with the hope of establishing a permanent settlement there. The first one, Captain L.A. Hagemeister, was a complete failure. And the second one, known as the "German Doctor" seemed to succeed temporarily in establishing a Russian foothold on the Island to Kauai. He was granted ownership of nearly half of the sandalwood of the Island and the right to establish control of half of Kawai if he would help King Tamori, of Kauai, defeat Kamehameha and establish him as the ruler of all the Islands. Scheffer, as the "German Doctor" was called, soon built a fort in Kauai. During this period, (in about 1816), the Russians who were captured on the Spanish land claims in California and were imprisoned for two years, were brought by an American Captain to Kauai. These refugees, Cossacks, Aleuts and Russians were put to work as slaves to cultivate taro. They were, therefore, the first white slaves in Hawaii. When King Tamori's request for military aid was rejected by Moscow, he ordered Scheffer off the Island, but he refused to leave. The king then, on the advice of the British and the Americans, no doubt, trained his guns on the Russian fort. Dr. Scheffer and his men abandoned the fort to escape to the ship in the bay. The last one to leave, it is claimed was the Orthodox priest, who returned to the fort for the Chalice and the Host, but left the censer behind. Scheffer escaped, and Russian thus failed to establish foothold in Hawaii. The censer, it seems, is still used in church services in Hawaii.

Wolansky, Rev. Iwan, 1857-1926 arrived in 1884 from Western Ukraine to serve as missionary among the Ukrainian Catholic miners, and other laborers in the United States. He established residence in Pennsylvania and visited centres where Ukrainian workers were concentrated travelling as far west as Colorado and Minnesota. In 1896 after travelling to Brazil to investigate on the spot the suitability of the Parana region for settlement by the Ukrainian peasants, he reported in the negative and this turned the tide of Ukrainian immigration from Brazil to Western Canada, and to the Dakotas and some went to Hawaii. Regrettably while visiting Brazil his wife contracted yellow fever and died in Rio de Janairo. He later returned to the Western Ukraine.

Appendix II

The Ardan Questionnaire:
(Please reply to the following questions)

1. What is the name of the plantation where you are working and the name of the owner and the manager?

2. How many of our countrymen work on that plantation — men, women, children — and from what villages and municipal districts (in the Ukraine) did they originate?

3. What kind of work do men, women and children perform?

4. What are the wages earned and how are the workers paid: by week, month, or any other way?

5. Where do workers live, buy their provisions, clothing and other needs and how much do they pay for them?

6. Give the exact time, place and name of the person by whom (give name) persons were punished or abused and maltreated?

7. Who persuaded the people to go to the Hawaiian Islands? What promises were made, and where did you get on board a ship?

8. Are there additional people arriving in Hawaii from Halychyna (Western Ukraine)?

9. Are there other people working with you, and to what ethnic group do they belong?

10. Please give your correct address.

Appendix III

Abstracts from petitions of workers who came to Hawaii from Manchuria.
                              —(National Archives, Washington, D.C.)

Собранием руских рабочих из числа
ста пятидесяти (150) человек
решено подать эту петицию
Его Кифу

Всем выборная комисия и подписываетса.
6⁻ Декабря 1910.

Члены комисии: Буря, В. Василев,
М. Либиск, Болдинг, Окунев,
Ивинчи. М. Кацмаки

Honolulu Harbor at Nuuanu Street, in the early 1890's.

Appendix IV

Partial Lists of Immigrants from Western Ukraine to arrive in Hawaii in October of 1898.
From the village of Kossiw:
Chuprynski, Petro, 48; Maryanna, 40; Stefan, 24; Iwan, 16; Anna, 14; Joseph, 11.
Czornyj, Hnat, 24; Kuprowski, Julian, 38; Frank, 35; Julia, 9; Antoni, 5
Fitkalo, Iwan 48; Maryya, 37; Dmytro 15; Oleksa, 8; Kirilo, 23.
Kowal, Iwan, 28; Karolina, 27; Anna, 4 mo.
Kowal, Iwan, 40; Theodora, 23; Hanuska, 18; Warwara, 13; Joseph, 3; Natalia, 6 mo.
Melnyk, Danylo, 30; Stefan 15.
Petriw, Ilko, 31; Malanka, 23; Pawlo, 5; Irena, 8 mo.
Petriw, Danylo, 32; Marya, 28.
Staszkiw, Iwan, 28, Anna, 26; Starzynski, Toma, 18; Swec, Iwan, 32; Rolski, Iwan, 29.
Chorney, Mikolaj, 33; Marya, 36; Pawlo, 9; Juliana, 5 mo.
Rygieljo, Michael, 40; Anna, 40; Petro, 12; Michael, 10; Onufrey, 7; Hnat, 6 weeks.
Sztynik, Feliks, 49; Tekla, 47; Kaszia, 19.
Yakimishyn, Ewdocha, 48; Anna, 26.

From the Village of Slobidka Dzurynska

Andruchiw, Iwan (20); Wozny, Theodore, (28); Pundyk, Maksym, Mr. and Mrs. and Antonia, (20), Joseph, (9), and John, (4); Tymkow, Wasyl (20) and family; Klachek Simon, (45), wife and three daughters; Florkiw, Stafan, (24) and Anna, (20); Sadoveyj, Stefan, (24); Wierzbicki, Fabian; (20); Bilowus, Gregorey, (26); Prus, Iwan, (24); Florkiw, Constantyn, (26); Luchka, Oleksa, (19); Garkus, Joachim, (20); Yanchyk, Audrej, (17); Durbaniuk, Roman, (24).

Bibliography

Research for the *Hawaiian Ordeal* was carried out in the following institutions:
Bishop's Museum, Honolulu, Hi.
Hilo Public Library, Hilo, Hi.
National Archives, Washington, D.C.
Public Archives of Canada, Ottawa
Lahaina Public Library, Lahina, Maui.
Library of Congress, Washington, D.C.
St. Andrews College Library, Winnipeg, Manitoba
University of Hawaii Library, Honolulu, Hi.
University of Manitoba Library, Winnipeg, Manitoba
University of Winnipeg Library, Winnipeg, Manitoba.
Winnipeg Public Library.

Magazines, Periodicals and Reports

Board of Immigration Reports
Hawaiian Annual, 1911
Hilo Tribune, April, 1899
Honolulu Advertiser
International Labor Office
Information Bulletin: United Nations
Pacific Commercial Advertiser No. 8655
Paradise of the Pacific, 1912
Star-Bulletin, Honolulu, 1985
Svoboda, Mt. Carmel, Pa., 1897-1910
The San Francisco Examiner, July 1899
The Friend, Honolulu, 1906
Washington Times July 1910

Aller, Curtis. *Labor Relations in the Hawaiian Sugar Industry.* Berkley Ca. 1957.
Bachynsky, Julian. *Ukrainian Immigration to the United States of America.* (Ukr.) Lviv, 1914.
Bancroft, H.H. *History of Alaska 1730-1885.* New York: Antiquarian Press Ltd., 1959.
Chevigny, Hector. *Lord of Alaska.* New York: Viking Press, 1942.
Chisholm, Craig. *Hawaiian Hiking Trails.* Beaverton, Oregon: The Touchstone Press, 1975.
Chumer, Wasyl A. *Collected Reminiscences of the First Ukrainian Settlers in Canada, 1891-1951.* Winnipeg; The author, 1942.
Chyz, Jar. "Ukrainian Immigration to Hawaii" *The Narodna Volja Alamanac.* Scranton, Pa. 1926.
Czumer, William A. *Recollections About the Life of the First Ukrainian Settlers in Canada.* (Louis T. Laychuk Translation). Edmonton: Canadian Institute of Ukrainian Studies, 1981.
Daws, Gavan. *Shoal of Time: A History of the Hawaiian Island.* MacMillan and Company, 1968.
Doroshenko, D. *History of Ukraine.* Translated from Ukrainian by Hanna Keller. Edmonton: The Institute Press, 1939.
Dunn, Richard S. *Sugar and Slaves: The Rise of the Planters Class in the English West Indies, 1624-1713.* Williamsburg, Va., 1922.
Du Puy, W.A. *Hawaii and the Race Problem.* Washington, D.C.; United States Printing Office, 1932.
Dutkiewicz, Henry J.T. "Main Aspects of the Polish Peasant Immigration to North America from Austrian Poland Between the years 1863 and 1910." M.A. thesis, University of Ottawa, 1958.
Fuchs, Lawrence. *Hawaii Pono: A Social History.* New York: Harcourt, Brace . . . 1961.

Hayashida, Ronald and Davis Kittelson. "The Odessay of Nicholas Russel." *The Hawaiian Journal of History.* June 11, 1977.

Herman, Bernard L. "The Caucasian Minority". *Social Progress in Hawaii Vol. XIV.* Honolulu: Sociology Club, University of Hawaii, 1950.

Horman, B. *Germans in Hawaii.* New York: Doubleday and Company Inc., 1975.

Ios'ko, Mikhail. *Nicholas Sudzylowsky Russel.* Minsk: Lenin Publishing Institute, 1976.

Kane, Robert S. *Hawaii A to Z.* New York: Doubleday and Company Inc., 1975.

Keller, W. Phillip. *Hawaiian Interlude: More Travels of the Tortoise.* London: Jarrolds, 1973.

Kennan, George. *Siberia and the Exile System.* (2 Vol.) New York: 1891.

Kohn, Hans. *Pan-Slavism: Its History and Ideology;* New York: Vintage Books, 1960.

Kraus, Bob. "Now the Russians Claim the First President of Hawaii." *Honolulu Advertiser,* March 28, 1969.

Kubijovych, V. *Encyclopedia of Ukraine.* Vol. 1 Toronto: University Press.

Latham, Edward. (ed.) *Statehood of Hawaii and Alaska.* New York: The H.W. Wilson and Company, 1952.

Lehr, John Campbell. *The Process and Pattern of Ukrainian Rural Settlement in Western Canada, 1891--1914.* Doctoral Thesis, University of Manitoba, Winnipeg, 1978.

Lengyel, Emil. *Siberia.* New York: Garden City Publishing Co., 1943.

Lensen, George A. (ed.) *Russia's Eastward Expansion.* Englewood Cliffs N.J.: Prentice Hall Inc., 1968.

Leschever, Barnett D. *Getting to Know Hawaii.* London: Longmans, 1959.

Lind, Andrew W. *Hawaii's People.* Honolulu: The University Press of Hawaii, 1955.

Lineberry, William P. *The New States: Alaska and Hawaii.* New York: The H.W. Wilson Co., 1963.

Loomis, Albertine. *Grapes of Canaan: Hawaii 1820.* Honolulu: Hawaiian Mission, Children's Society, 1966.

Luke, Sir Harry. *Islands of the Pacific.* London. George G. Harrop and Co., Ltd., 1962.

Lyon, Fred. *A Week in Winaley's World: Hawaii.* New York: Crowell-Collier Press, 1970.

Maude, H.E. *Of Islands and Men: Studies in Pacific History.* Melbourne. Oxford University Press, 1968.

McLaren, Nancy Austin. *Russian Immigration: Hawaii* M.A. thesis, Honolulu: The University of Hawaii Press, 1951.

Mirchuk, I. *Ukraine and Its People.* Munich: Ukrainian Free University Press, 1949.

Myshuha, Dr. Luke. *Jubilee Book.* Jersey City: Ukrainian National Association, 1936.

Oleskiw, Joseph. *O Emigratsiyj,* About Emigration. Lviv: Prosvita Society, 1895.

Nordyke, Eleanor C. *The People of Hawaii.* Honolulu: University of Hawaii Press, 1977.

Roland, Donald. *The United States and the Contract Labor Question in Hawaii, 1862-1900."* Pacific Historical Review, 1933.

Rudnyckyj, J.B. *From My Sabbatical Diary, 1970-71.* Winnipeg: Pub. by the author, 1972.

Russell, Dr. Nicholas K. "Olaa". *The Hawaiian Annual, 1899. Honolulu: Thos. G. Thrum Publisher, 1899.*

Shrewsbury-Mesick, Lillian. "The Galician Failure and the Christmas Tree", *Paradise of the Pacific.* Honolulu, 1912.

Sonevytska, Olha (ed.). *The Chortkiv District A Collection of Memoirs and Historical Data.* New York: The Shevchenko Scientific Society, 1974.

Spector, Ivar. *An Introduction to Russian History and Culture.* New York: D. Van Nostrand Co., Inc., 1961.

Stechishhn, M. I. "The Ukrainian Brotherhood in California." *Ukrainian Voice Almanac.* Winnipeg, 1940.

Tate, Merze. *The United States and the Hawaiian Kingdom: A Political History.* Yale University Press.

Woodcock, George and Ivan Avakumovic. *The Doukhobors.* Toronto and New York: Oxford University Press, 1968.

Woodcock, George. *Canada and the Canadians.* Toronto. Oxford Press, 1970.

Index